INFIDELITY

Other Books by
Brian Richard Boylan

THE NEW HEART

and with
Charles Weller, M.D.

THE NEW WAY TO LIVE
WITH DIABETES

HOW TO LIVE WITH
HYPOGLYCEMIA

PRENTICE-HALL, INC.
ENGLEWOOD CLIFFS, NEW JERSEY

INFIDELITY

BY
BRIAN RICHARD BOYLAN

Infidelity by Brian Richard Boylan

© 1971 by Brian Richard Boylan

Copyright under International and Pan American Copyright Conventions

All rights reserved. No part of this book may be reproduced in any form or by any means, except for the inclusion of brief quotations in a review, without permission in writing from the publisher.

Library of Congress Catalog Card Number: 71-129629

Printed in the United States of America • T

ISBN 0-13-464362-3
Prentice-Hall International, Inc., London
Prentice-Hall of Australia, Pty. Ltd., Sydney
Prentice-Hall of Canada, Ltd., Toronto
Prentice-Hall of India Private Ltd., New Delhi
Prentice-Hall of Japan, Inc., Tokyo

PREFACE

There are three ways to write about marriage. One is a handbook of rules and suggestions for surviving in marriage. Another is an objective report on what goes wrong in marriage and why. This second approach is especially popular if it is filled with opinions by marriage experts—psychologists, psychiatrists, marriage counselors, clergymen. The third approach is for an author to listen, not to the experts, but to married persons themselves about what is good and bad in marriage.

The third approach is the one followed in this book. The ideas, opinions, and conclusions come from the married persons who have had to look beyond marriage for fulfillment of unmet needs. The marriage experts are deliberately ignored, except when they comment on their own marriages. The reason for this is that the only time a married person can be trusted to speak the truth is when he is talking about his own marriage. The moment he discusses someone else's marriage, he becomes an observer and his opinion is colored by morality, religion, contemporary social standards, laws, and what he thinks others expect of him.

A psychiatrist says one thing to a patient involved in marital difficulties but something much different about his own marriage when he is chatting with a close friend. The attorney who quotes the law to his divorce clients may sound like a different man when he is candidly explaining what is wrong with his own marriage. The pastor is expected to praise the sanctity of marriage to couples on the verge of splitting up, even when he knows that his own wife is so unhappy that she is turning to other men. Another irony is that some effective marriage counselors are homosexuals.

There is nothing strange about people speaking alternately out of two sides of their mouths, one for public consumption, the other for their friends. Man has elevated hypocrisy to such an art that its practitioners are proud of their ability to say with conviction the exact opposite of what they believe.

This book was conceived many years ago after I had observed how married persons were in the habit of discussing their marriages one way in public but differently in private. The men and women who admit privately to infidelity often proclaim their marital bliss in public.

Another observation that prompted this book was that married persons are eager to confide their disillusionment and fears to a sympathetic ear, but they do not want advice or moral censure. What they want is the chance to talk about what is bothering them in marriage without being blasted by a sermon in response. In short, many of them want a psychiatrist but do not want the social stigma of actually consulting one or the accompanying burden.

Years of listening and observing the marked differences between public pronouncement and private confession finally led me to start making notes and thinking about a systematic study of why husbands and wives look outside of marriage for unmet needs, what they find, and the impact of this search on their marriages.

This book is based on the words and thoughts of the men and women who engage in infidelity. In no way is it a scholarly study. There are no tables, no carefully calculated percentages, and no extensive bibliography to indicate my own scholarship. I have indeed read many books on the subject, as well as articles in journals and in popular magazines. This massive research, however, has not overly influenced the book because the words of the husbands and wives I listened to are sufficiently eloquent.

Instead of surveying thousands of married couples to discover their opinions on infidelity, I have instead sought out those who practise infidelity. They have been interviewed individually and, wherever possible, I have gathered the views of both partners in a marriage. The language in many of the cases may appear crude, but I have tried to retain the actual words. If anything, the language has been toned down a whit.

I talked to approximately 350 persons over a period of five years. Of these, perhaps one hundred were interviewed intensively, that is, for two hours or more—often spread out over several days.

Each interviewee was guaranteed anonymity, and for this reason each case has been fictionalized just enough to disguise it. The words, however, are those of the individuals involved.

If anyone whom I have not interviewed recognizes a case history, then that is a proof of the universality of infidelity. In several instances, cases were virtually duplicated, and I have picked the most representative for illustration.

Brian Richard Boylan

CONTENTS

	PREFACE	v
	PROLOGUE	1
One	A NEW DEFINITION OF INFIDELITY	5
Two	THE MEN WHO PRACTISE INFIDELITY	31
Three	THE WOMEN WHO PRACTISE INFIDELITY	53
Four	THE PRACTICAL STRATEGY OF INFIDELITY	73
Five	THE SOCIAL-LEGAL JUNGLE OF INFIDELITY	95
Six	PERMISSIVE INFIDELITY	101
Seven	THE IMPACT OF INFIDELITY ON MARRIAGE AND DIVORCE	105
Eight	THE UBIQUITOUS THIRD PARTY—THE LAWYER	135
Nine	DIVORCE AND THE INDIVIDUAL	143
Ten	PRACTICAL COMPLICATIONS OF DIVORCE	153
Eleven	THE COMING REVOLUTION IN MARRIAGE	161
	EPILOGUE	175

INFIDELITY

Prologue

One of the saddest tragedies of the human condition is the long, painful awakening of married men and women to the realization that the Ideal Marriage is a cruel hoax, a self-perpetuated bad joke. And it is typical of the human rational process to repeat to our children all the bromides, platitudes, and slogans we have discovered to be false.

And even when we have learned by bitter experience to distrust emotional judgments, we continue to *hope* that all will be for the best. Nowhere is this more obvious than in marriage. All around us are yelling, bitching, battling examples proving that a man and woman can live together in peace only rarely, and then only with enormous compromise. Yet we rush romantically into marriage. When we discover that we were wrong and the marriage ends in failure, do we profit from the example? Of course not. We cast about for a new partner to marry, always hoping that this time things will be different. And even when we're miserable in marriage, we ram into our children's heads the concept of Ideal Marriage.

Two people in love are ecstatically happy, and they want to extend that happiness into the future. In a typically human gesture, they burn bridges and seal up escape routes by binding themselves legally and religiously to be all things to one another for the rest of their lives. If they're happy today, happier than yesterday, then they certainly will be happier still tomorrow.

To the unmarried or the unhappily married, the prospect of spending every day and night with a beloved can drive a person dangerously close to giddiness. Love unquestionably is man's ultimate sensuous experience. The person in love is traditionally the happiest man or woman alive; when out of love, he is bitter, disillusioned, and cynical. Large numbers of people continually fall in love; if they are at all attractive to the opposite sex, the knowledge that there may be another love waiting around the corner can soften the pang from the wreckage of the current affair. And there are some who have rigorously determined never again to expose themselves to the tumultuousness of love.

"I don't fall in love," Britain's Lord Arran wrote at age fifty-eight in *Punch,* "And that makes me sleep well. No doubt my sons fall in love, but that is their private agony and I can only sit back and pray for their maturity and their daily increasing likeness (spiritual) to myself."

If these words infuriate the romantics, they will bring smiles of recognition and agreement to ex-lovers and retired lovers. Because falling in love is such a stupendous experience in human life, falling out of love or losing love can be embarrassing and humiliating.

No matter how violent the passion, how strong the love before marriage, years of daily living together can shatter premarital illusions about ideal marriage. He belches after supper. She dislikes making love with the lights on or when the children are around. He can't stand schedules. She prefers to dress plainly around the house and sleep in flannel granny gowns. He prefers hiking and camping to social entertaining. She is bored by housework and lets the dishes and washing pile up for a few days. He likes jazz. She studied to be a concert pianist. He has regular partners for tennis, golf, and squash. She discusses money problems at supper. He wants a dog. She prefers a cat.

Ideal marriage usually is replaced rapidly by realistic marriage as two individuals learn they must compromise continually for the marriage to be a success. Marriage, stripped of ideals, hopes, and illusions, is simply a compromise. If the partners can compromise with dignity, it is possible for them to be able to live together long enough to become genuinely fond—as well as tolerant—of one another.

Many couples, however, refuse to acknowledge that their ideals have not come to pass. They daily reassure one another with proclamations of eternal love while subconsciously they wonder what has happened to the dream. When these disappointments reach a painful degree, and when the partners in a marriage can no longer compromise, infidelity makes its debut.

Chapter One

A NEW DEFINITION OF INFIDELITY

Most married persons define infidelity as adultery, the physical act of extramarital intercourse. Those whose opinions and vocabularies are shaped by popular magazines coyly refer to this activity as "cheating." But infidelity as it actually is practised by married men and women is much more extensive and involved than simple adultery. In addition to sexual infidelity, there is emotional infidelity and psychological infidelity, plus many lesser forms.

A more accurate definition of infidelity is that it takes place whenever a married person repeatedly has to look outside the marriage for a need not fulfilled by the person's spouse. *Need* is the key to this definition, for it indicates the importance of certain needs in everyone's life. It is the rare couple who can be all things to one another. The gratifications which people expect from marriage are so varied and demanding that the absence or denial of just one can send the deprived partner stumbling into infidelity—that is, looking for this need from another.

The thought that infidelity is the offspring of need is enough to make moralists and marital "experts" gag. Widespread acceptance of such an idea would force the popular newspaper psychologists and advice dispensers to draft a new batch of platitudes for their correspondents. Judging from the contents of these columns and the women's magazines, infidelity is the hottest issue today, more debated than the Pill and more inflammatory than marijuana.

This phenomenon is not too difficult to understand because infidelity represents traditional morality's last stand against what has been overstated as "The Sexual Revolution." Premarital sex has indeed been liberated, thanks in part to the widespread availability of oral contraceptives. Now the sacred institution of marriage is threatened by increasing public and personal tolerance of extramarital sex.

Such fears are, of course, scare tactics on the part of the upholders of the status quo. It is true that sexual infidelity is probably increasing, but we are aware of this because emotional and psychological infidelity are practised freely and without conscience rumblings, and practitioners of all forms of infidelity are less bashful today. Since sin is no longer such a dominant factor in American morality and sexuality, the married person who commits infidelity may feel uncomfortable or perhaps even guilty, but rarely does he expect Divine Lightning to smite him dead.

American traditionalists regard sexual fidelity in marriage (monogamy) with the same reverence in which they hold the American flag and belief in God. To question any of these publicly is reprehensible and will bring down upon the questioner the wrath of society. The extent of this national lack of humor toward sacred subjects can be measured by the ferocity shown toward flag-burners, atheists, and, to a lesser extent, public personalities who openly defy monogamy. When, in the mid-1960's, disgust with what they considered to be an obscene war in Vietnam caused many Americans to burn the flag in protest, the outcry against them was immediate and fierce. Responding to this patriotic wrath, Congress immediately passed harsh laws, and judges handed out stiff sentences to the culprits. Americans reacted with similar violence toward those who had successfully urged the Supreme Court to ban prayer and Bible teaching in public schools. Then, as 1969 approached, the sexual revolution felt the attack of the traditionalists. A well-organized assault on sex education in schools forced many school boards to revoke these programs. The foaming fury of the antisex forces was almost identical in intensity to that directed toward flag-burners and Bible-banners.

But the amusing aspect of the outcry on behalf of monogamy is that many of its loudest champions have privately practised what they publicly damn. Our national double standard is nowhere more obvious than in this delicate subject. While researching this book, I often found that the man or woman who loudly denounced infidelity in public would confide in private to having engaged in emotional, psychological, and sexual infidelities.

Taking the new definition of infidelity as a standard, does this mean that the wife who has an afterwork drink with her boss is unfaithful? Or that the husband who takes another woman to lunch is unfaithful? Of course not, but when such companionship is deliberately sought out because something is missing in the marriage, then infidelity must be considered. Thus, the woman who goes out after work with her boss because he is brighter and wittier than her husband, and because her boss is more attentive and solicitous of her opinions, probably is involved in one phase of infidelity. She may never go to bed with him or with any man other than her husband, yet she is unfaithful to the monogamous standard.

Such a woman is Marge, thirty-two, a legal secretary. Marge insists that she still loves her husband, Frank, a thirty-seven-year-old high school economics teacher. "Frank's world begins and ends at the high school, and while I'm interested in his work and want to share everything with him, I discovered shortly after our second daughter was born that I needed other adult conversation. As soon as the little one was in school, I went out looking for a job. Frank didn't mind so much because he could see that I was getting bored and also the money would help supplement his teacher's salary." Marge was lucky to have worked as a legal secretary before she married Frank, so it took her only two interviews before she accepted a job as secretary to Mark, an articulate lawyer one year younger than Marge. Although Mark was separated from his wife, he never made an overt pass at Marge, but frequently asked her to join him for a working lunch or for a relaxing drink after work. Had Mark shown any sexual interest in her, Marge could have handled him. But instead she felt that she was the one who was pursuing this relationship.

"I would never dream of being unfaithful to Frank . . . well, that is, I might dream about it but I'd never really do anything. It's just that Mark is such a nice man with a delightful sense of humor. I never feel tense or strained around him. I feel I can be myself with him, something I don't really feel with Frank. Oh sure, when we're making love, I feel very close to Frank, but the rest of the time I feel that his mind is in a textbook or a classroom and that I'm just an animated decoration around the house."

Marge was not sexually naïve when she met Frank, and she honestly rated his boudoir techniques as "fair to adequate." However, she said that her love for him prohibited her from going to bed with another, perhaps sexier, man.

What no one could tell Marge, yet what is obvious, is that her involvement with her boss was one of the preliminary forms of infidelity. She was turning regularly to him for needs which Frank was not supplying. If these needs were strong enough, sooner or later she probably would drift into stronger forms of infidelity.

The fact that infidelity does exist in so many different forms is not so shocking as the refusal of the participants to recognize what is happening to them. If an obvious desire to flirt is understood by the flirter as stemming from something that is missing in marriage, then he or she can perhaps do something to correct it in the marriage or, if not, then openly recognize what the flirting indicates.

If the new definition of infidelity is valid, and if infidelity is indeed a common deviation from monogamy, it is logical to inquire whether infidelity might be beneficial rather than harmful to a marriage. Couples who live by the new definition agree that different phases of infidelity can serve as a safety valve to keep healthy marriages free from the pressures of constant companionship. Research for this book has shown that while a large percentage of couples accept the new definition and lose little sleep over what takes place without their knowledge, few openly encourage sexual infidelity. The infidelity they accept is anything that does not disrupt their marriages, alienate their spouses, or publicly embarrass them.

Ralph and Susan are not a typical couple in that they each know that the other occasionally is unfaithful . . . but they don't discuss it. Both have been married once before, both are in their thirties, and they have two children plus one from Susan's earlier marriage. They live in a modest apartment in a suburb near a large city. Ralph's work takes him into the city every day, and Susan, who is a free-lance artist, visits there on an average of three times a week.

"Ralph and I occasionally spend separate evenings away

from home—sometimes for the entire night," Susan said. "I don't worry about whether he's being unfaithful, but I certainly would be annoyed if my friends saw him necking heavily with another girl. As long as he's polite to me and kind to the children, I'm content. Once or twice he's been moody and irritable for a few days, and I suspect at such times that he may have gotten involved with someone else. During these spells I leave him alone and the clouds usually pass within a week or two. I know wives who, if their husbands behaved that way, would leap on their backs immediately and bear down. That's silly, because such pressure will only drive an unfaithful husband deeper into his shell or else provoke him to a violent outburst. The last thing I want is to force Ralph to think of all the reasons he has to be angry or unhappy with me, then throw them in my face in defense against my needling.

"I must say that Ralph returns the courtesy on those rare occasions when I saddle him with the kids for a night. Once, a few months back, I returned home at 4 A.M., after a thoroughly satisfying evening with an old friend. Ralph was still awake and he wanted to make love. I was so emotionally and sexually wrung out that I told him I probably wouldn't be able to participate with enough enthusiasm to make it worth his effort. He could have gotten snotty but instead he just smiled and promised to try again in a few nights. He did, and I was more than ready for him.

"He never asked me about that night, just as I have not questioned him about his disappearances, and I think our marriage is pleasanter this way. Imagine the hell we both would be going through if we kept possessive guard over each other, demanding an accounting for every hour spent away from home."

While this example is not typical, it does represent the changing attitude which has become more common during the 1960's. Unlike Ralph and Susan, those couples who do tolerate infidelity usually require that it be disguised or passed off as something else. The important point is that they are tolerating it.

It is difficult to draw sharp boundaries between the three common forms of marital infidelity—sexual, emotional, and psychological—for they frequently overlap. While only one may represent the need missing from the marriage, the other two usually enter at some point. Wives who first look outside their marriages for emotional or psychological needs may find themselves caught up in sexual involvements. Fran, thirty-eight, a career woman whose only child was almost out of high school, found that while she had been emotionally attracted to other men in recent years, her husband's sexual performance was enough to keep her reasonably satisfied. However, her involvement with Mike, a slightly younger divorced engineer, rapidly escalated to a situation where she was reluctantly eager to carry the emotional relationship over into the physical. Mike pressured her for several nights unsuccessfully. After one such evening, Fran returned home and hungrily sought out her husband as soon as they got into bed. He was tired, but he consented.

"I wanted desperately to be taken and driven to the brink of sexual insanity," Fran recalls. "My husband instead did his usual competent job, but I kept fantasying about being laid by Mike. Ordinarily, I respond rather rapidly to my husband's lovemaking, but on this occasion I had to fake it."

The following day, Fran was jittery and irritable. Finally, she called Mike and asked him to meet her after work. "After three drinks, I suggested going back to his apartment. Apparently he had given up on my going to bed with him, for he treated me with complete politeness and deference, only kissing me gently in the cab. We sat in his apartment for at least an hour, while he mixed drinks, played his stereo, showed me some new books, and generally behaved like an adolescent out for the first time with a girl. Even after we snuggled together on the couch and started to kiss seriously, he still expected to be rebuffed. I was terribly excited and wanted to drag him off to bed, but I let him slowly get the idea that he was seducing me. Once he got this into his head, it became easy for me to cooperate enthusiastically with him. For an experienced man, he was awfully clumsy getting me undressed and into bed. I think he was unsure of himself. Had he just suggested that we both undress and get into bed, I would have responded immediately. Instead, I had to wait through his careful undressing of me. He did pretty well until he came to my pantie girdle, and that really threw him. Later, he told me that most men regard these things as obstacles to sex. I had never thought about that since I always removed my clothes before getting into bed with my husband, and he never had to struggle.

"What really puzzled me was Mike's refusal to articulate any of his questions or uncertainties. I'm not sure I could have answered them directly had he asked, but I would have tried. For example, it would seem to me that contraception is something that a couple about to make love should be very frank about. But Mike only jumped out of bed and fished in his pants for his wallet before he returned triumphantly with a condom. I didn't want to spoil his moment of triumph by telling him that I had inserted my diaphragm earlier, before I left the office to meet him.

"Well, at last we made love, but Mike was so excited that he exploded after half a minute. He was terribly upset about this, but I was able to reassure him that it was the feeling and tenderness that counted with me. About an hour later, Mike revived enough to give me one of the most satisfying sexual experiences I have ever had. He took me from complete relaxation and, within minutes, led me over the brink. By the time he let loose, I was on my second orgasm, and we both came together."

It is popularly believed that unfaithful husbands seek sexual gratification first, then find emotional and psychological fulfillment with women who are good in bed. If anything, this generalization is true only as an exception to the rule. Men who are emotionally compatible with their wives often will put up with an indifferent sexual relationship for years before venturing into infidelity. This is not true, of course, when the marital sex life is either nonexistent or surrounded by painful demands, bartering, or loss of dignity.

An unusual example of a man who was driven into infidelity by a wife whom he loved is Mark, a forty-two-year-old geologist. Mark had been monogamous for fifteen years with Helen, and they rarely fought seriously over anything. But when it came time for sex, Mark was disappointed.

"During the early months of our marriage, I kept suggesting that we try different positions, and I was eager to make love whenever the mood struck us. Not Helen. Once the marriage settled down, it was only on Friday or Saturday nights, because she didn't have to get up early the following morning. Now that the children are growing up, it is only on Friday nights . . . when she is in the mood. The trouble is that I have to take my wife out to a party, or else entertain, wine, and dine her before she is willing to make love. On those rare occasions—no more than twice monthly now— the ritual follows the manual to the letter.

"I cannot touch her until we are in our bedroom, usually after 1 A.M., with the door shut. Then I am permitted to kiss her and even fondle her breasts. I very much like to undress her, but in recent years she has insisted on doing this herself—in the bathroom. As soon as she begins to respond to my lovemaking, she runs for the bathroom and spends at least twenty minutes undressing, washing, perfuming herself, and putting on a sexy negligee. By the time she emerges and is ready for the grand seduction, I've usually lost interest and I'm ready to fall asleep. But this is where the work begins.

"Once Helen is in bed, with the lights out and the bedroom door locked, I then am permitted to seduce her. This means kissing, fondling, licking, manipulating, and otherwise doing everything possible to turn her on sexually. After an hour of this, I'm invariably worn out, but I persist, for if I don't, she'll be restless all night and bitchy the next day. When I'm lucky, that is, when she's slightly drunk, she turns on and is ready to consummate the whole dreary business. At that point she grabs me in the groin to indicate her readiness. Whether I'm ready or not, I'm expected to jump on top and pump away. Once she has had her orgasm she becomes impatient as hell with me. Remember that I have had to get it up on a minute's notice, but goddamn it, I want my jollies too, especially after working so hard to satisfy her."

After fifteen years of marriage, Mark found himself at a convention where a local call girl tempted him sorely. Not wishing to patronize a prostitute, but definitely aroused, Mark began to think of how much nicer sex might be with a different woman. Within six months, he was in bed with a twenty-seven-year-old co-worker whose sexual behavior was the antithesis of Helen's.

Had Mark been basically unhappy with Helen, the sexual infidelity probably would have led him immediately into emotional infidelity. But he and Helen got along excellently and understood one another.

The climax of this story is almost unbelievable, but it deserves to be told, if only because it is so atypical. After a few experiences in bed with other women, Mark behaved like a scientist and reported his findings to Helen in the form of a technical paper. He analyzed what was wrong with their sexual life, described his findings in extramural research, and announced his conclusions: either Helen cooperate in improving their sexual relationship or he would continue to bed down with other women, possibly to the detriment of their marriage. Helen was outraged but she recognized the soundness of Mark's argument, and she agreed to try to spice up their bedtime activities.

This case is detailed to show a variation from the routine pattern of male infidelity. Unlike Mark, most husbands interviewed for this book indicated that emotional and psychological infidelity came long before adultery.

Jerry, thirty-eight, a technical writer who has been married twice, summarizes his experiences:

"In both of my marriages, once it became evident that there were large gaps in our mutual understanding, I subconsciously began flirting with other women. Not to take them to bed, but just to establish a relationship which was missing for me at home. And in both marriages, the moment I found another woman who really seemed to match me temperamentally and emotionally, I would fall in love. When this happened, it was only days before I would be in bed with the girl. I find that emotional involvement leads directly to sexual fulfillment. If it doesn't, there is something wrong with the relationship, and it should be (and usually is) broken off."

The difficulty in generalizing about infidelity is that the popularly supposed preferences of husbands and wives often are reversed. The man who strays may really be looking for a mother more than a sexual temptress, just as the unfaithful wife may be craving power rather than someone to dominate her. The stereotype has it that men stray for sexual satisfaction, women for emotional. The situations are so often reversed that the stereotypes are worthless.

Sexual Infidelity

Sexual infidelity ("What men call gallantry and the gods adultery," in Byron's definition) is the best-known symptom of an unhealthy marriage. It is the type of infidelity that leaps into the minds of marriage counselors, psychiatrists, clergymen, and social workers when they try to assess a crumbling marriage. These marital authorities are, of course, aware of the other forms of infidelity, as is anyone who closely examines the incredibly complex pressures surrounding a man and woman who are expected to be all things to one another until death do them part.

But the great forum for marital problems is not the psychiatrist's office or the pastor's rectory. It is the columns of the popular magazines and newspapers, especially *The Reader's Digest, Cosmopolitan, Ladies' Home Journal,* and *McCall's*—most of them read by middle-class housewives—that carry at least one article per issue extolling the sanctity of mariage or roundly damning any attempt to deviate from monogamy.

Marital folklore in America holds that sexual infidelity is a peculiarly male sin. The only time it is acknowledged to be practised by a wife is when the woman is utterly without redeeming social importance. But even the most cursory examination of modern marriage indicates that sexual unhappiness is as responsible for wandering wives as it is for unfaithful husbands.

This discrepancy between folklore and reality can be traced to the fact that, until recently, most articles about sexual infidelity have been written by men. Female sexuality has always interested men, and they always are regarding it as something new, a phenomenon produced by innovations such as oral contraceptives, relaxed moral standards, short skirts, equality between the sexes, or the decline of puritanism.

Rarely do male writers credit wives' sexual drives to their husbands' sexual incompetence. Whenever men discover that women are looking beyond their husbands for sexual gratification, they blame it on some new influence, not on dissatisfaction with husbandly sexual ability. It is worthwhile to remember that while monogamy may seem to be beneficial to the wife, it has been husbands who have trumpeted its innate virtuousness from the pulpit, in the press, and in the legislatures.

The theory that women have started enjoying orgasms only since getting the right to vote or wearing pants in public is ludicrous, but it still is seriously advanced by many men. The male human is so defensive and guilt-ridden about his own sexuality that for him to admit that his wife is bored by his boudoir virtuosity is unthinkable. So when she starts exhibiting uneasiness or when she becomes sexually unfaithful, his only defense is to blame it on the Pill or changing social standards.

A parallel can be drawn with the wife who blames her husband's infidelity on his insatiable, animalistic lust rather than on her own inability or refusal to meet him halfway sexually.

The Roots of Infidelity

Although it would seem that the basic reasons for infidelity would be too numerous to categorize, the interviews conducted for this book all point to one outstanding cause: premarital misconceptions about what marriage would be, and postmarital disillusionment. One couple, Ed and Francine, illustrate this misunderstanding:

First of all, what did you think marriage would be like when you got engaged?

ED: Well, I was twenty-one when I proposed to Francine, and she was the first girl I really loved so much that I wanted to spend years and years with her. We petted heavily in college, and after we were engaged, we got so carried away three or four times that we actually made love. But these episodes were just titillating rather than indicative of what was to come. We were smothered with guilt since we had agreed to save it until we were married. Our premarital lovemaking was, naturally, disastrous, for neither of us had had any experience. So it really didn't interfere with my illusions. I thought that once we were able to be with one another all day and all night our love would grow and grow to the point where I would be incapable of even looking at another woman. During our engagement, I found myself frequently leering at other girls, including one whom I had dated before meeting Francine and who, since I had become engaged, had become much more tempting. I kept telling myself that once I was spending every night making ecstatic love to the one woman I really loved that I'd be too drained to think of other women.

FRANCINE: I saw marriage as being a beautiful experience, the essence of love, in which my darling and I would be transported onto a cloud through a mingling of the physical and spiritual oneness we would achieve. It sounds rather corny now, but that's what I thought then. I didn't physically enjoy those first premarital sexual experiences, perhaps because I was too hung up with guilt and thoughts about what my parents would say. Also, I had grown up reading all those newspaper columnists who insist that nice girls save it for marriage. Maybe I was even subconsciously refusing to enjoy it before marriage. I was moony as hell over Ed, but not enough to miss a few flaws in his behavior. However, I knew that if he really loved me, he'd be willing to change and improve once I pointed them out to him after we were married. I must admit, incidentally, that while I held back from enjoying the premarital sexual episodes, Ed really turned me on when we were just necking. I kept thinking how marvelous it would be to blend this beautiful spiritual love with a oneness of body.

How soon after your marriage did your ideals change?

ED: It must have taken me at least six months to consciously realize that I wasn't getting what I expected out of marriage . . . certainly not in bed and not in the daily living routine. Actually, I think my ideal was shattered before we returned from the honeymoon. Even though we spent three weeks at a mountain resort, I thought we'd be making love around the clock, pausing only for meals. I discovered, however, that this wasn't Francine's idea of a honeymoon. Also, I discovered that I had my sexual limitations. What really bothered me at first was that she and I get interested at different times. I am sensuous in the morning, wanting to make long and leisurely love, but Francine is a pop-out-of-bed girl who jumps into the shower, eats breakfast, and gets going on her daily activities. On the other hand, after a long day, I really want nothing more than to collapse into bed and fall asleep. Francine is just getting warmed up at night, and she is ready to swing until daybreak. But it wasn't just sex that was different from what I had expected. It was the daily living pattern, a series of constant compromises. I never expected to be the boss or any of that nonsense, but I was amazed at the number of times we were on the verge of quarreling over some petty little detail. Adjusting yourself to the mood of another person is a traumatic experience!

FRANCINE: It must have been at least six months before I realized how my premarital ideals were changing. Ed was much more difficult than I had imagined and he balked over the silliest things. For example, on about the third night of our honeymoon, he took a bath and didn't clean out the ring in the tub afterwards. I didn't say anything, but I was shocked, for this is something that everyone should do. However, after the third or fourth time it happened, I asked him very nicely if he would do this little thing for me. He laughed, said yes, and promptly forgot about it. After several months of marriage, I really lit into him and told him how inconsiderate he was to make me clean up after his mess that way. I was stunned at his reaction. We had our first fight that night, and later, when I was feeling affectionate in bed, he turned his back on me. As for sex, I think I'm a normal girl, but I have found Ed very difficult to communicate with concerning what really stimulates me. He is so sensitive about my making suggestions, and as a result there have been many nights when I've lain awake for hours, unsatisfied and hurt. Although at the beginning of our marriage Ed was very chivalrous about taking the necessary contraceptive precautions, after a while he started insisting that I get fitted for a diaphragm. I explained to him that this was repugnant to me, but he insisted. Now, whenever we plan to make love and I go off to the bathroom to prepare, he whines at me for taking so long, claiming that I'm deliberately stalling so that he'll lose interest and fall asleep.

Ed and Francine were interviewed six years after they were married. Both seemed unhappy at the time and both expressed a definite interest in extramarital activities, although neither had experimented so far. Within another year, they separated, divorced, and both eventually remarried.

Overfamiliarity

If familiarity breeds contempt, what will marriage do to two individuals? How can a wife take seriously the public pronouncements of a husband she regards as a jackass and a rotten lover? How much respect can a man hold for a wife whom he knows is an incurable slob and an emotional vampire?

The only answer to the potential mutual destructiveness of marriage is for both partners to be damned sure they respect one another, then for them to do everything possible to sustain that respect. A man and a woman who share the same bed, bathroom, and bank account can easily ruin one another. This is seen in the outpourings of personal degradation that accompany so many divorces. Also, it is seen in the emotional blackmail which keeps many rotten marriages together.

Men and women have destroyed their partners professionally, socially, and even personally by revealing unsavory personal traits or predilections.

Although most couples who remain married work out a treaty not to reveal certain aspects of personal lives, a mate's characteristic which is impossible to tolerate may lead a married partner into infidelity while shunning divorce. Some unfaithful married persons will heavily involve themselves with outside partners but will never leave out of feelings of guilt or protectiveness.

Generally, men tend to be more protective than women. A man will feel guilty over his wife's alcoholism and will not leave her. Even if she starts sleeping with other men, he may feel so guilty at having failed her in bed that to seek a divorce would be admitting his own failure.

But the woman whose husband is thrown in jail, committed to a mental institution, or caught in another woman's bed is less likely to be charitable, particularly if he is no longer able to support her and the family.

Support is a key idea, for even the most sentimental woman will become the bitch of steel when there is no money for food and the creditors start sniffing at the door.

Infidelity vs. Divorce

Despite the progress in divorce reform throughout the country, it still is a punitive process that severely hurts both parties, benefiting only the lawyers. The unhappily married man with children often will look at his divorced friends and decide that the legal horrors are much worse than staying in his marriage and indulging in infidelity.

The intensity of infidelity often is an accurate barometer of the storminess of a marriage. The unhappily married man or woman tends to become heavily involved with an extramarital partner, falling seriously in love. The person whose marriage is relatively pleasant, however, usually will try not to become seriously dependent on the outside partner. This is not difficult to understand, for the person disappointed in marriage will look eagerly for someone else to supply what the spouse can't or won't. On the other hand, a married person who is relatively satisfied may indulge in an occasional spree to gratify some unmet need, but such an individual doesn't need or want the total dependency that the miserably married seek. Ralph and Susan, the couple described earlier, who each occasionally entertain unfaithful experiences, are examples of the casually unfaithful. Bern and Ronny, who remain married only because their religion and their families frown on divorce, are at the other end of the pendulum.

Bern is a forty-two-year-old adolescent, falling in love with almost every woman he takes to bed more than once. A highly successful public relations executive, Bern admits that each love affair is more grandiose than the previous. His pattern is almost routine. A handsome, witty man, he has no trouble attracting stimulating women in his office and wherever he travels. He is one of the few nonglib men who can walk into a cocktail party and walk out with a bed partner.

But Bern is not interested in a quick lay. He wants to fall in love, and he succeeds in doing so regularly. If the affair is at all serious, Bern falls in love and usually is able to produce the same effect in his partner. His next step is to bemoan his marriage of fourteen years with Ronny, a hard-bitten, tough woman who also is in the public relations business and who, he tells his inamorata of the moment, loves to castrate him at every chance. Bern's pattern is almost fatalistic as he leads his girl friend to the point where she really thinks she can pry him away from his wife. Then the big struggle begins, accompanied by tears, fights, reconciliations, and ultimately, splitting up. Bern preys on those girls who themselves have no compunction against stealing another woman's husband, especially when he is there for the plucking.

Bern really is there for the plucking, but to do so requires patience and stamina beyond the reach of most of his girl friends. He insists that if only his one, true love of the moment would be just a bit more patient and understanding, he would leave Ronny and marry her.

Bern's credibility is questionable because he has the untidy habit of letting Ronny know that he is having an affair, and with whom. More than one of his mistresses have been accosted over the phone or in person by Bern's outraged wife. After each of these scenes, Bern shuffles his feet and apologizes abjectly to his girl friend, but then returns home on the last train.

Even when describing these incidents, Bern tells them with a boyish laugh and a toss of his curly hair. He admits that on more than one occasion his wife has physically assaulted him. Ronny's favorite strategy is to aim a vigorous kick in the direction of Bern's groin and hope it will connect. Once after such a kick Bern retaliated, slapping Ronny's face so hard that he blackened her eye.

Ronny is somewhat different from Bern's description. Although she is indeed hard-nosed and practical, she is not that eager to hang onto Bern. "When that bastard is making enough to support the children, I'll be more than happy to let him go," she insists. Her fear is that if they are divorced, Bern will continue to spend money like water and be unable to support their four children. Although she earns a tidy sum as an art consultant to several

PR agencies, she does not want to be stuck with supporting the children by herself.

Ronny has experimented with infidelity, actually falling in love twice. But both the men she loved were married, and both were enmeshed in complicated marital difficulties. Also, she decided that neither one would make an adequate husband.

Ronny had one wild three-month orgy with a single man three years her junior whom she describes as being the most sexually satisfying creature she had ever met.

"When Bob and I walked into his apartment, we would shut the door very gently, then savagely tear off our clothes. Being alone with him meant only one thing—making love. We did it on his couch, on his floor, in his bed, on his sailboat, in the woods, and even once in the ski lift. I did not love Bob, but every moment I was with him I was hungry for him. We stopped seeing each other regularly three years ago, but the other night I met him at a cocktail party, and within minutes we were making love in our hostess's bedroom."

Bern hasn't divorced Ronny because of his fear of what it will cost him, both in money and emotional turmoil. And Ronny is reluctant to be stuck alone with the children, depending on Bern to support the family. Both were raised as Catholics although neither has practised the religion since shortly after their marriage (when contraceptive necessities drove them both from the Church). Yet there are strong family pressures against their getting a divorce. When Bern moved out for three weeks and sent a multiple letter to all his family announcing his intention to divorce Ronny, his mother arrived at his hotel room two days later and tongue-lashed him so severely that he moved back to his house the next day. The fact that his mother threatened to disinherit him from a substantial pile of money had nothing to do with his return, he insists.

Temptations

Modern marriage is beset by occupational and environmental temptations to infidelity. Assuming there are unmet needs in the marriage, the restless spouse can find innumerable temptations on the job, in the office, on the road, or even in the home community. Husbands can be tempted by secretaries, fellow workers, and women they meet while traveling, should they be interested in straying. And wives today run into hordes of eager men (most of them married but available) in social groups, study clubs, or recreational organizations. Should the wife work at a full-time job, the temptations are increased considerably.

For all but the extremely timid, infidelity beckons its tempting finger. No man or woman who wants to be unfaithful need look very far.

An ironic aspect of infidelity is that men who are surrounded by potential recipients of their affections often assume guiltily that their wives are denied equal opportunity. This is absurd, for the infidelity-prone woman has but to join the community theater, the church committee, a discussion club, or any of the adult-education courses to find droves of men. Unless she is so miserable in her marriage that she wants another husband, the average wife may be looking for flirtation or something more serious—and she doesn't care whether the man is married or not. In many respects, it is safer if he is married, for then neither partner can make excessive demands for time on the other.

The community theater provides a fertile ground for infidelity, since the ambience associated with it requires that its members be relaxed and witty about sexual dalliance. One theater in a populous midwest suburb is notorious for breeding affairs among its members. A male member summarized the role of the theater: "Hell, most of those who turn out regularly are interested in getting laid, unless they're fags or middle-aged couples looking for a mutual hobby."

Miranda, a forty-two-year-old housewife with almost-adult children, threw herself into an East Coast fencing club, "in order to get rid of some excess weight." Within a few lessons, it became obvious to the instructor that Miranda was looking for more than simple exercise. When paired off with a man, she lunged and thrust with such force that the instructor had to keep reminding her that the sport of fencing requires feather-like *touchés*. Miranda often took great glee in ramming her foil against a man's chest and causing a bruise. "There, let your wife see that and try to explain it to her," she would shout.

Miranda was married to a fifty-year-old importer who also was a fulltime bore. Although she was not especially beautiful, Miranda had preserved a slim, well-coordinated body, and she was a good match for beginning male fencers. Two weeks after she started her lessons, Christophe, her thirty-two-year-old teacher, invited her out for a drink to discuss her progress.

"Miranda, you don't want to learn how to fence . . . you want to screw every man you run up against," he told her. Miranda professed shock at first, then later admitted that this was true. Christophe took her to his apartment where, according to Miranda, "he screwed the living pants off of me."

The bored housewife really needs to look no farther than her community for sexual or emotional stimulation. The man who is surrounded by voluptuous young things at the office can suddenly find his wife spending four nights a week away from home, locked into meaningful discussions with an available man.

Accidental Infidelity

Accidental infidelity is simply the result of placing an infidelity-prone person into a slightly different environment with another sexually attracted person. That is, the husband or wife who is interested in sexual infidelity might hold back because of fear of detection. But when an opportunity comes along to spend several nights away from spouse and home, the stage is set for accidental infidelity. For example, the traveling husband who attends a convention or sales meeting in another city meets a fellow worker whom he has leered at surreptitiously back at the office. She also is alone in a strange town and delighted to see a familiar face. They both are attracted to one another. A blend of alcohol, a romantic setting, and infidelity proneness can result in accidental infidelity.

This form of sexual infidelity is very popular with the conscience-ridden married persons who don't want to hurt their mates. They can blame it on "an accident," and responsibility for the episode slips easily out of their fingers.

Insidious Infidelity

Married men and women who have been involved in serious affairs testify that the moment other forms of infidelity joined sexual infidelity, they were hooked. Several described how what started out to be just a casual sexual affair between two friends insidiously developed into an interdependency, escalating to a full-blown love affair.

These same individuals report that it is possible to keep an affair on a strictly sexual plane, but that requires a coolness and detachment that can be very destructive to the other person. When a friendship moves into bed, the two partners often are looking rather vaguely for lovers. Each one wants someone who will be more and mean more than the spouse. Should the sexual experience be unusually gratifying or stimulating, it will be repeated.

With every repetition, the cord of interdependency tightens, especially as the two find out how similar are their thoughts, prejudices, and past experiences.

The liaison becomes a full-blown love affair the moment the man and woman start rearranging their lives to spend as much time as possible with one another. The affair may not even be a sexual one for it to be full-blown, although this is the exception to the rule. Sometimes a couple can be overwhelmingly attracted to one another, but their sexual life isn't particularly stimulating and they spend little time together in bed. There are other affairs where it is physically very difficult for the two to find a place to make love. This is particularly true in small communities and suburbs. However, those with strong sex drives manage to come together.

Chapter Two

THE MEN WHO PRACTISE INFIDELITY

Although it might seem that unfaithful men and women would have widely different reasons for their actions, detailed questioning indicates that such an assumption is not true. Men and women are unfaithful for essentially the same reasons. Each is trying to fulfill a need unmet in marriage. And each is defying the monogamous standard, an unrealistic, unworkable, and totally absurd standard. It is the actions of the men and women who practise infidelity that show monogamy to be such a rotted corpse.

The reasons why men and women practise infidelity may be similar, but because of the differences in the roles of husband and wife the sexes will be separated, as it were.

MEN AND MONOGAMY

One basic assumption can be made about unfaithful husbands: Their marriages may have deteriorated but are not yet intolerable. When a marriage is unbearable, it usually ends in divorce. Of course, there are exceptions to this rule. Anyone who is familiar with infidelity can rattle off examples of husbands who violently hate their wives yet stay married because of religious restrictions, family pressure, the fear of distressing the children, too little money or over-indebtedness, and—in a surprising number of cases—an almost masochistic need to be tyrannized by a wife.

But setting aside the obvious exceptions, it is safe to generalize that a husband engaged in infidelity is not necessarily a miserable husband. True, he may well hop from infidelity to divorce if his marriage is unsound. But the very fact that he returns to his wife regularly is an indication that his marriage may be fulfilling some needs. It may also indicate that an intelligent, cunning woman has yet to grab him by the nose and pull him away from his wife.

A theory cherished by wronged wives and moralists alike is that the human male is just like the male of other animal species, biologically equipped with an insatiable lust for constant copulation with a variety of females. What this theory ignores is that in those animal species where the male is sexually rambunctious, the female in heat is receptive to any and all available males, or at least to the male who is strongest and is capable of overcoming in combat all competitors.

The reasonably detached observer of modern marriage will agree that deviations from monogamy are as common among women as among men. When conception was uncontrollable and when society ostracized the unfaithful wife but not the husband, women tended to be more cautious about engaging in extramarital affairs.

Marital Backgrounds

Unfaithful husbands come from a variety of marital backgrounds. Some wander into infidelity early in their marriages, others wait for several years. Most of those interviewed indicated a single turning point in their marriages which led them into infidelity.

In some instances, the turning point was a dramatic one, shutting the door on past monogamy. Examples of this include wives suddenly shunning or ignoring them after the birth of a baby; a radical change in religious beliefs by one partner; a distinct change between the engagement and the marriage, such as a sudden decline from neatness to slovenliness, or from intense sexuality to indifference in bed; or wifely unhappiness over a change in job or career.

There is the husband whose wife doesn't understand him—a much sneered at phrase that unfortunately is all too true.

There is the man whose wife is a good mother, an excellent housekeeper, but is sexually cold toward him.

In researching this book, I have talked to husbands who want to give their wives more love and affection than they seem to want.

I have seen husbands nagged and needled out of their marriages.

I have seen men searching desperately for a woman who will accept their love and give them back the affection and admiration that their wives deny them.

And I have watched potentially good marriages disintegrate because an ambitious Other Woman was willing to provide just the ego stimulation and sexual excitement that a preoccupied wife carelessly denied her husband.

Inadequate Preparation for Marriage

Few married men are prepared for their first marriages. Those who marry young often are sexually inexperienced, while those who marry later seem incapable of adjusting to the compromises necessary in living with a wife. This observation applies to the infidelity-prone male; that is, the restless, inquisitive man. The husband who is grateful that a woman would marry him and is willing to make any sacrifice to keep her happy is not infidelity-prone and therefore not the subject of this book.

The man who marries young may have had sexual experiences, but they usually have been fleeting, quick copulations. Emotionally, he may have been involved with other women, but broke off with them for a variety of reasons. The man who marries young usually marries the first woman who appeals to him sensually, sexually, emotionally, intellectually, and psychologically. Thinking that he has found the ideal combination in one girl, he gallops into marriage. This man wants to marry and feels that if he doesn't, he will be a reject on the social market. He wants a woman who will satisfy him in bed and also be a presentable social companion. He is uncertain of himself and wants to acquire that passport to respectability in business and social affairs: *a wife*. He knows that employers prefer to hire married men, and he often feels like a social leper at parties where his friends are snuggly paired off with their wives or fiancées or steady dates.

As a result of these social and internal personal pressures, he is in the market for a wife. Every girl he dates is carefully examined and tested. He wants to get married so badly that he proposes to the first girl who seems to fill all the qualifications.

If he is less than a prize catch, he may find himself with two or three rejected proposals, which only make him work harder to disguise his faults and impress the next girl. The marriage-conscious young man ultimately finds a girl who is fetched with him, or who is so anxious to get married herself that she temporarily puts aside his obvious defects, confident of remedying them once the honeymoon is over.

This young man enters marriage with a host of preconceptions and ideals about what marriage will be, and invariably he is disappointed. Often, he is sexually disappointed on the honeymoon when he discovers that marital sex requires much more work than the premarital quickie in the back seat of his car or on her couch. He discovers that his bride has a sexual appetite of her own that is distinctly different from his. She needs to be gently and elaborately aroused to the point where she is ready for intercourse. His own concept of sex has been that several hot Hollywood kisses and some kneading of her breasts are the only preliminaries to a passionate coupling.

Assuming that the young groom wants to satisfy his wife in bed, and assuming that he is conversant with the popular marriage manuals, he will follow their instructions. However, he often finds that once the union is legal, a certain indefinable excitement disappears. The girl that he occasionally made passionate love to before their marriage suddenly is a wife who now requires an elaborate romantic and sexual buildup before she is ready for intercourse.

Many men who married young report that their patience was frayed on their honeymoons and that they ultimately said to hell with the lengthy preliminaries and simply hopped on.

Jon is a man who complained bitterly about his honeymoon experiences. "Christ, every time we went to bed together before we were married, Eileen was as hot as a firecracker. I couldn't get it in fast enough to suit her. Of course, I didn't last very long, but her squirmings and wrigglings made me think that I had satisfied her completely. On our wedding night, everything changed. We checked into a resort hotel, drank a bottle of champagne, and then went through the standard ritual. You know, she went into the bathroom for an hour while I watched television. When she came out, she was wearing this elaborate bedtime outfit. I'd have preferred to make it on the couch two minutes after we walked in, but Eileen had to follow the formula. When she came out of the bathroom, I was sitting in front of the TV in my shorts, smoking a cigar. Women get all decked out on their wedding nights, but what are we grooms supposed to wear? I quickly threw the cigar out the window into the hotel pool and ran into the bathroom, where I put on the pajamas I had bought just for this night. I always sleep in my shorts, but that seemed sorta gauche on our wedding night. When I came out, Eileen was lying across the bed in a seductive pose. I promptly jumped onto the bed and started kissing her, the way we had throughout our engagement. We had only made love three times before we were married, so I followed my instincts and removed her nightgown. No sooner was she completely naked (and me too) than I got it between the eyes. 'Please play with me, Jon,' she insisted. Well, I played with her for two goddamned hours before she finally let me in. Afterwards, I fell asleep immediately, but she kept cuddling up against me. Finally, late in the night, she awoke me by kissing my neck and stroking me. She begged me to make love to her, but I thought about how much effort it would take and promptly went back to sleep."

Sex seems to be the strongest surprise for those who marry young. Men who marry after years of experience with women report that sex is not nearly so troublesome as working out a daily living compromise.

The man who marries after having survived the trauma of postadolescence and the social pressures to marry in the early twenties probably has lived as a bachelor for several years. There are some men who from their earliest years successfully shack up with women until they finally decide to marry. The majority of men who reach their late twenties without marrying, however, are not successful rakes.

From this corps we must immediately banish medical students, professional scholars, and other monastically-inclined young men. The man who marries after the temptation-filled years of the early twenties usually has a self-confidence with women that his early-marrying fellows lack. He is the man who has been able to score successfully with girls without having become emotionally involved. Also, he is sure enough of himself that he does not have to worry about where his next affair will come from. He can take pleasure without demanding love, and he can find love without demanding that it be sealed and guaranteed in writing forever.

However, such a man frequently marries for the first time a woman who has proved to be an excellent bed companion without seeming possessive. Assuming he is sexually sophisticated, this man often enters marriage without understanding what it means to live with a woman every day.

The man who marries after living with a woman can confuse an off-and-on situation with full-time partnership. Jerold, a successful actor, had a two-year affair with Virginia, during which they often spent days together in one another's apartment. When it first started, Jerold and Virginia indulged at his place. Then, to offset the suspicions of his neighbors, Jerold went to Virginia's apartment. They were intensely in love, and every weekend was a sexual frenzy. They both were in their early thirties and had agreed that this would be a casual affair. One night after Virginia dated an old boy friend, Jerold showed up very late and insisted that they marry. They did the following Saturday and jointly moved all their things into Jerold's apartment.

Until their marriage, they essentially had gone their separate ways. Jerold's evenings were spent at the theater, while Virginia was involved with writing a novel which an agent had told her to rewrite so that he could submit it to a publisher.

At first, their nights were spent in ardent sexual togetherness. Within months, however, Jerold was back on the stage and Virginia was working on her novel.

Although they got along well in bed, their hours in a mutual home were marred by certain individual differences. For example, Jerold was a late riser and late worker. He rarely got up before noon but would come home after an evening at the theater and stay up until 3 A.M. or later.

Virginia, on the other hand, liked to get to sleep early and get up early. The morning and afternoon hours were the time of her peak creativity.

The conflict first started three weeks after they were married. Virginia jumped out of bed at 8 A.M. and began writing. Several hours later, Jerold got up, showered and shaved, then walked in on Virginia as she was typing. He was full of love and wanted to carry her back to the bedroom for an afternoon of sexual debauchery. But Virginia was steaming along and didn't want to be bothered.

Differences rapidly appeared. Virginia liked to shower immediately before going to bed, but Jerold preferred to shower and shave in the morning. He would start to make love to Virginia, only to have her jump up and run off for a ten-minute shower session.

Also, Jerold was a slob, whereas Virginia was compulsively neat. Jerold would heave his clothes into a corner at night as he climbed into bed, only to watch Virginia retrieve them and put them into a hamper.

Jerold and Virginia had everything going for them in the beginning, but as the months and years passed, they found out that they really got on one another's nerves. Each had lived alone too long to be happy about making major compromises in living, eating, and sleeping habits. To recite the differences is to make them seem trivial, but the effects on their marriage were very evident.

The need for compromise has driven many otherwise pleasant marriages onto the rocks. The best compromisers are those who enjoy having part of their lives carefully directed by another. However, even such passive individuals occasionally like to have their own way.

Combine irritation with having to compromise over differences in emotional and sexual compatibility, and even the closest lovers will draw apart. A man wants total gratification from marriage and he rarely gets it. He may not engage in any form of infidelity, but that is generally because of fear, not lack of desire. There is something to be said for the time-honored old custom of selecting a wife for her practical advantages, but not for love. Love is such a fragile flower that subjecting it to the overexposure of marriage seems the surest way to kill it.

This is not to say that husbands do not love their wives. Many of them, whether they are unfaithful or not, enjoy a gentle, warm love for their wives. However, few such men claim that the hot, passionate love is still raging. And this is one of the reasons for infidelity.

When a husband sees that romantic passion slipping and fading as his marriage moves into low gear, he feels cheated or deprived. He often attempts to revive it with his wife, sometimes successfully. But by this time, the turning point of the marriage has been reached, and this unfulfilled romantic need drives him outside the marriage to other women.

One conclusion that can be drawn from extensive interviews of unfaithful husbands is the high percentage who first sought love, not necessarily involved with sex. It is a common platitude that the unfaithful husband is just oversexed. But this is not true. The cooling off of love and affection at home sends many more men into infidelity than does simple lust.

Many of these same love-hungry husbands point out that when they first sought love, affection, and warmth from another woman, they had no intention of getting sexually involved. And men who have had previous affairs are not always panting to get into bed with other women—particularly when their wives are adequate lovers.

One of the best illustrations of how marriage drains passionate love is the comparison unfaithful husbands make between their sexual performances with their wives and with their lovers.

Men who are capable of virtuoso performances in bed with other women admit to being duds in the marital bed. Of course not all such men have psyches strong enough to enable them to admit to any sexual weakness. The more self-confident the man, however, the readier he will admit that his domestic sexual prowess is less than dazzling.

"I am unquestionably the worst lay when I'm in bed with my wife," Ted, a thirty-eight-year-old engineer reports. With other women, Ted is rated a superior lover, a consummate master of sexual technique. He is so effective in selecting suitable women, then turning them on, that one summer he discovered that three relatively detached, supposedly uninvolved companions had all fallen in love with him and were interested in marriage. Although Ted and his wife Lynn, share a warm love for each other, the sizzling passion of their engagement and early marriage departed with the arrival of their first child.

"I've always had some difficulty arousing Lynn, but

once I realized that the excitement was gone for good from our marriage, I guess I just stopped trying. Oh, I'll still work on her a bit, especially when she's really interested, but I just want to get it all over with as fast as possible—which makes me a rotten lover for Lynn. Perhaps I don't give a damn in the sack because I'm doing so well with other women. But I really think my sexual failure at home is because it's no longer fun to boff Lynn."

Ted's first episode of full-blown infidelity occurred when he was thirty, seven years after he and Lynn were married. The year before, he had had a quick sexual involvement with a distant cousin. Ted and she got pleasantly loaded at a party and ended up in bed at her apartment. Both Lynn and the other woman's husband were out of town. The session left Ted with a warm glow but without the love and affection he was subconsciously searching for. For his first intense affair, Ted became involved with a married woman, thus violating a tradition that married men have affairs with unmarried women.

THE SINGLE OTHER WOMAN

This tradition is understandable, for an unmarried lover (especially if she lives alone) provides the necessary place to meet sexually. Also, her hours are her own and she does not have to report back to a puzzled husband. Theoretically, she is available every night and weekends.

It is this precise availability that snags so many affairs. An unmarried woman makes herself totally available to her lover, who unfortunately has to return home every night. He might be able to fake a few all-night sessions away from home, and he usually manages to take off from home on a Saturday or Sunday for at least a few hours. But if he has children, he must spend at least part of the weekend with them—a fact that has been infuriating single women for many centuries.

Even when she has no great desire to marry the man, the single Other Woman rarely is happy with a part-time (in her opinion) lover. This unhappiness is communicated to the married man.

Married men who have affairs with single women admit that falling deeply in love with such a person is disastrous, if only because of the demands she will make on the man's time. It is a grossly imbalanced situation: He has complete access to her but she only can enjoy him when he is free.

Such affairs usually are controlled by the single woman, just as they usually are terminated by her. Her reaction to having to share her lover with his wife is to exercise power. She can pressure, tempt, or punish the man by simply withholding herself when he has time for her. In unpleasantly sticky affairs, she may flaunt her position as mistress under the wife's nose. She can, if really bitter, ruin her lover by carefully tormenting him by phone at his job and at home. She can throw screaming tantrums when they are together, especially when it is time for him to return home. She often encourages him to tell her all the sordid details of his marriage, sympathizing at first, but slowly, subtly using them to berate him for his weakness and stupidity at not getting out of the marriage immediately. Then, if he does make definite moves to leave his wife, the single Other Woman can urge him to act faster by suddenly becoming coy and hinting that she may not be available even if he does get a divorce.

These situations apply, of course, to the serious affair, not to the casual sexual encounter. Married men who have had extensive extramarital experience tend, after a few intense affairs, to look for women who will not become overly dependent on them and thus not make excessive demands.

Married Men and Married Women

Unfaithful husbands can also move in the direction of married women. Although they possess certain built-in disadvantages, to certain men a married woman is ideal as a love partner. Her time may be limited, and she may have to return home, but doing so, she is in no position to demand that her lover spend the night or weekends with her. The principal disadvantage to such a liaison between married persons is finding a place to meet and enjoy one another fully. This is a problem of such magnitude that lack of a ready solution turns off many affairs before they ever can get started. However, one of the partners may have a spouse who works late or travels frequently. Or there may be a convenient office where they can spend useful hours. Or one of the partners may have a single friend who is willing to let them use an apartment or a summer house.

The chief advantage cited by many men to having an affair with a married woman is not the freedom from demands to spend more time with her—although that ranks high on their lists—but rather the fact that a married woman is *experienced*. Not only is she acquainted with sexual techniques, but she knows some of the things that turn a man on or off.

When a married man tells a married woman that he doesn't feel like eating since he'll be obliged to wolf down a large supper when he returns home, she has enough sense to understand his point and not try to shame him into eating supper with her, as a single woman often will do.

A married woman knows the protocol of contraception

and is not likely to be coy or innocent about it at the last minute. This is a subject about which she has definite attitudes, and she doesn't waste valuable time pretending to be ignorant.

A married woman knows the importance of sex to a man and doesn't try to tease him to the breaking point. She wants it as much as he does. She doesn't play games with his psyche.

Married Men as Lovers

Women who have had extensive experience with men, and who are not interested in marrying every man they have an affair with, claim that married men can be better lovers than single men. That is, technically they tend to be more efficient than single men. But this is a generalization that would be difficult to support without a massive scientific investigation. However, the majority of such women interviewed for this book support this theory.

Their argument is very simple: A married man tries harder. A husband who is dissatisfied with his domestic sex life knows what it is he needs, and he is willing to do his damnedest to achieve it. When he finds a woman who responds to his physical attentions, he will work to bring her to complete sexual satisfaction. He has had experience with at least one woman, and he knows what he must do.

Making It

There are some men who make it extramaritally with little effort while there are others who try again and again but rarely succeed. The difference between these two types of married men seems to be one of self-confidence. If a man feels he is physically repulsive to women, he is likely to be defensive and uncertain in approaching them. Even if he is physically attractive, he may be in such doubt about his sexual capabilities that he will enter into an affair shyly, even apologetically. He is terrified of failing in bed. He dreads the prospect of getting a woman sexually aroused, then being unable to satisfy her because he ejaculates ten seconds after he has entered her.

Some married men never get over their timidity. They may engage in affairs, but they constantly are apologizing in advance to their partners for their sexual inadequacies. These men will spend an inordinate amount of time arousing a woman to the point of orgasm before entering her to protect themselves from the accusation of coming prematurely—an accusation that rarely occurs to their partners.

The self-confident male, on the other hand, knows that he can withstand the intense eroticism of copulation and delay ejaculation long enough to satisfy his partner.

Arnie is a forty-year-old bookkeeper who has had occasional affairs since he was twenty-eight. "Sure, I was worried about holding back when I first went to bed with Fiona. She turned me on so wildly that I knew I couldn't last five seconds once in her, so I tried to bring her almost to the point of orgasm before I entered her. While we were playing, she described a technique that one of her previous lovers used. He mentally put himself somewhere else while he was screwing. That is, when he felt his body taking over from his will, he immediately imagined himself stretched out on an isolated beach in the West Indies, listening to the waves lapping around his ankles. That way, he was able to delay his orgasm until after she had come. Well, I tried it and it worked! Ever since, I've been taking trips to the Caribbean or the Rockies at a crucial moment, but I've been able to hold off until Fiona was ready."

(There is nothing mysterious about the technique Arnie

used. It is taught by some physicians and psychiatrists to help men control and delay orgasm. It is a variation of self-hypnosis.)

Whether an unfaithful husband is successful or not with other women depends on many factors other than the sexual one. Some of the most active men are great seduction artists but perform less brilliantly in bed. And, in many cases, the man is looking for love and not necessarily sex. A husband who is strongly attracted to another woman, particularly if she is single, may well go along with her reluctance to make love. When the other woman is married, it is a bit more difficult for her to resist his sexual requests. For the most part, married men who are involved with married women tend to take sexual indulgence for granted.

Married Men Who Compulsively Fall in Love

This man is familiar to students of infidelity, for he is perpetually looking for and finding love, then botching it. He usually is attractive, charming, intelligent, and financially comfortable. His marriage may be dreadful but more often it is just dull and unpromising. This man is an easy mark for the single woman who decides to steal herself a husband. He'll agree with her and fall desperately in love. But unless his marriage is really unsatisfactory he will be very difficult to pry away from his wife.

This man can bounce from the wreckage of a traumatic affair right into a fresh involvement with an almost boyish eagerness. He throws himself into affairs, is quick to fall in love, then suffers wretchedly when his partner starts to pressure him and berate him for not leaving his wife.

His worst fault is that he implies to all his partners that he will leave his marriage imminently, when in reality he knows that his departure is still in the future.

One of this man's most endearing qualities is his willingness to receive as well as to give love. He will pour out large quantities of love to a woman and permit her to be equally loving. This give-and-take attitude is not overly common among married men, according to the women they have had affairs with.

And it is this charming trait that later infuriates his partners in infidelity, for they fall deeper in love with him than they ever would have with an aloof or selfish lover. The compulsive lover implies so much that an unmarried woman wants to hear that he suddenly finds himself no longer controlling the affair. While he has been talking about leaving the marriage and perhaps living with his new friend, she has jumped ahead several positions and is planning the wedding, furnishing their apartment, and introducing him to her relatives and friends with knowing nudges and winks.

THE MARRIAGE HOPPER

Somewhat like the married man who jumps from one affair to the next, the marriage hopper goes from one wife right into the arms of a second wife. He has more determination than the affair-jumper, for he actually gets out of an unsatisfactory marriage. However, no sooner is he out than he signs up for another lifetime relationship.

A few years ago, I spent some time at a company filled with creative men and women. The majority of both sexes had been divorced, but when it came to remarriage, the differences were startling. Every man, without exception, had quickly remarried, but only one woman out of thirteen divorcés had remarried. And all the divorced men had remarried within one year after the final legal decree.

This little group provides a microcosm of marriage, infidelity, divorce, and remarriage. The men who left their marriages often had someone else to go to, but the women who left were deserting the world of togetherness for loneliness. And that is what nearly every divorcée reports she has found—unvarnished loneliness. Loneliness, however, often is preferable to misery.

Why do divorced men eagerly run to another marriage so quickly? The obvious answers—that they need companionship, care, and love—are not totally satisfactory. There are men who demand their "freedom" from a wife, yet voluntarily surrender this freedom immediately. It may be that the human male is less able to adapt to loneliness than the female. Or perhaps he is reluctant to jump back into the world of dating and courting. Whatever his reason for remarrying—and there are as many reasons as there are remarriages—divorced men tend to remarry within a year or two after their divorce.

The exceptions to this rule are so few that they stand out. The first is the man who is paying so much support and alimony that he "cannot afford to remarry." This generally means that he is reluctant to get burned in marriage a second time, or that he has not yet met and fallen in love with a woman who was willing to work so they could afford to live together.

Another exception is the divorced man who really enjoys his independence and prefers living alone, seeing women and other men when he chooses. This man often seems hardened and obstinate to women who would like to move in with him full time. In some ways he is inflexible and will not let a casual affair—one that he does not regard as having long-term potential—grow to a degree of passion that will become impossible to shut off. This man may well remarry after several years of living by himself, but it will be only when he is ready.

Men Who Have Remarried

It might be thought that men who have remarried would have different thoughts about infidelity, but that is not necessarily true. Of such men interviewed for this book, approximately half reported infidelities during their second marriage. These infidelities, it should be noted, did not occur during the early years of the second marriage, except in a handful of cases. Remarried men who have indulged in infidelities during the first marriage generally are more tolerant and understanding than men still married to the first wife. They report that their second wives are more sensitive about the subject, perhaps because so many of these wives conducted affairs with them while they still were married to their first wives.

Not surprisingly, the second wives who understand infidelity better maintain a much stricter watch over their husbands. Remarried men report great difficulty in conducting infidelity. Their second wives are, in many instances, prepared to anticipate the urge to look to another woman.

Josh has been married to Lola, his second wife, for six years. He has had casual sexual encounters with some old girl friends, but no serious infidelities. However, he thinks that one explosive affair may be just around the corner.

"There's a girl I've met socially—she's a friend of some people at the office—and we seem to be moving rapidly toward each other. She's separated and knows that I'm married. I know she wants a good, warm relationship at this point; I doubt that she is thinking about remarriage, but I don't doubt that she could move that way with the right man. And frankly, after six years of marriage to Lola, I'm getting just a bit bored. The sparkle and the passion have definitely gone, although we still love each other very warmly. Our sex life is excellent—I doubt that I could find a better bed partner than Lola. She was spared the traditional American upbringing which riddles children with guilt about sex. Lola is easy to arouse and easy to satisfy. As a result, she'll generally have at least one bone-rattling orgasm each time we make love. We do have a rule in bed—no quickies. If it's worth doing, we prefer to do it thoroughly and to the complete satisfaction of both. When just one is excited, the other will use the hand or the mouth to provide quick satisfaction."

With such a heady sex life, how can Josh find time or emotional energy to conduct a full-blown extramarital affair?

"Good sex in marriage is great, but there are other important elements, such as personality and mutual interests. Lola is a bit on the argumentative side. She likes to challenge whatever I say. Sometimes this is just to get a brisk discussion going, which I don't mind. But other times I have the feeling she is challenging me just to knock me off balance. It's the classical situation: She will eagerly accept and agree with a point made by a stranger, even though I have been making the same point for months.

"Also, Lola has her photographic interests, and she can be quite obnoxious in assuming that those are the only ones of importance in the house. She'll yell at me to turn down the goddamned stereo when she's concentrating on printing pictures, but she gets huffy when I suggest that her goddamned chemicals are stinking up the bathroom.

"Also, Lola is possessive to the point of jealousy. I didn't mind this for a while, since my first wife was just the opposite. However, the moment she knows that I'm going to be spending time away from her with other women, she pulls every string to come along, or telephone me, or pick me up. And when she can't, she gets mean as hell. Lola can be surly when something is gnawing at her.

She'll start off by speaking softly for several minutes as though nothing was wrong. Then she turns and lashes out at me verbally. In any argument, she's never wrong and I'm always thoughtless, inconsiderate, or cunningly cruel."

Josh admits that his main interest in the new woman is emotional rather than sexual. However, he knows that if an affair gets started, they both will rapidly add sex. He doesn't intellectually want to have an affair, because he knows the drain it will put on his emotions. He also knows the time it will consume. However, Josh is most worried about Lola's reactions. He does not want to jeopardize the marvelous sex life he has at home, but he is missing certain emotional and psychological gratifications in his second marriage. One of these, he recognizes, is his need to be admired and deferred to by a woman, which Lola never does.

"I don't want a girl to fawn over me—that's usually phony anyway. But I would like to feel important occasionally. Sometimes with Lola I even get the idea that to her I'm simply a stud in bed and a household decoration out of bed."

Lola, who was interviewed separately, was suspicious that Josh was getting restless.

"I recognize that he's pulling back from me. I hope it's just temporary, because I'm not about to let him get involved with another woman. He was halfway out of his first marriage when I came along, we had an ecstatic affair, and I pried him loose from that bitch he was married to. She never knew how to use Josh. God, what a lover that man is!"

Lola is hurt that Josh may be looking to other women for emotional satisfaction. She regards him as a sweet but undisciplined adolescent whom she is perpetually having to bring back into line.

"I really love Josh and I really want him to be happy.

But he seems so restless, so distant these last few months."

Josh thought that a full-blown affair might ultimately help his marriage, but Lola was convinced that such an affair would destroy it. If she found out that Josh was in love with another woman, she'd know that she had failed. Also, her instincts of vengeance would drive her to find a man with whom to have an ostentatious affair under Josh's nose.

Lola has some friends who practise *permissive infidelity,* that is, each partner feels free to get involved with people outside the marriage, but they don't necessarily tell one another about the affairs.

Although she told Josh before they were married that someday, maybe when she was drunk, she might enjoy a group sex experience, Lola now has changed her mind. And she cannot abide the thought of Josh's making love to another woman. She knows that if he becomes emotionally involved, it will only be a matter of days before he is in bed with a girl.

In many ways, Lola is a composite of second wives. Her views on infidelity are theirs: Infidelity is a legitimate weapon in the hands of a single girl prying a husband out of a bad marriage, but it is wicked and immoral when used by another woman on their own marriages.

At this point we are only concerned with the attitudes of wives toward their husbands' infidelities, not what they think about being unfaithful themselves. That will be discussed in the next chapter.

The only significant conclusion that can be drawn from a study of men who practise infidelity is that the majority of them are looking for emotional and psychological—as well as sexual—fulfillment. Their affairs range from the casual, sexual bout between close friends to sexless but emotionally torrid affairs to complete involvement.

Chapter Three

THE WOMEN WHO PRACTISE INFIDELITY

"No male has any right to talk about the extent of female response because he can't have the vaguest idea of what he is talking about."

William H. Masters, M.D.

On the basis of extensive interviews, it appears that married women practise infidelity in its various forms just as much as married men, although married women take longer to *admit* to unfaithful desires. The broadened definition of infidelity as something that happens any time a married person has to look outside the marriage for an unfulfilled need is especially pertinent to women. A married woman may stoutly deny any infidelity as long as it means adultery, but when the psychological and emotional aspects are mentioned, a surprising number readily admit to them.

Women traditionally have suffered from the double standard which winks at husbands who play around but heaves stones at women taken in adultery. Therefore, they have a built-in reluctance to admit to what may be very strong feelings. Even today, a woman who gets caught sleeping with another man is considered much more reprehensible than her similarly inclined husband. A divorce gets particularly nasty when a husband challenges his wife's fitness as a mother because she has had sexual relations with another man. The fact that he has been in and out of bed dozens of times with other women, and even been caught at it, somehow doesn't earn quite the moral censure that an adulterous wife receives. Most divorce-court judges are male, and despite the traditional male claim that the husband always loses in a divorce, when both parties are equally guilty, judges tend to be more severe toward women. In the American judicial system, the bench is not always occupied by the wisest men, but frequently by clever politicians and party hacks, men of limited intelligence who suffer from all the common prejudices of the herd. Confronted with a wife who has flaunted the double system, many judges react as husbands traditionally do and reach for the stones.

The women who practise infidelity will engage in the emotional and psychological aspects of it long before they experiment sexually, unless, of course, they are in a rotten marriage. Like their husbands, these wives gradually become disenchanted with the marital myth, and channel their energies into clubs, groups, and other friends. Not acknowledging any sexual interests, such women will flirt outrageously with interesting males but retreat at first when a man pursues.

Wives who work regularly and are unencumbered with children can develop unfaithful desires almost as rapidly as their husbands, particularly if their social and recreational interests are different. The couple that works together and plays together will have a difficult time breaking loose to conduct any meaningful relationships with others. Of course, as the years of marriage wear on, most such couples gradually drift apart.

A wife with children is hampered during the years when the children are small, but if she already has made up her mind to develop a life for herself with friends of her own, she will manage.

For example, Bev has become very active in the PTA in her suburban community, despite the fact that her youngest child is six months old. Her other child is in the second grade, and Bev freely admits that the second one may have been a mistake. Her husband is a stockbroker who takes his work home with him every night and who is bored to tears by the PTA. Bev tried to coax him into coming to meetings, but he said he was so turned off by the people involved that he'd rather stay at home and baby-sit while catching up on his paper work. On those nights when he is tied up in town, Bev hires a baby-sitter or coaxes her older sister into watching the children.

"This is very important to me, and if George isn't interested, that's too bad—I'll go without him. We have a very large PTA and it gives me the chance to express myself forcefully. Most of the men I meet there are married, while many of the male teachers are very definitely unmarried. Curiously, I find myself spending more time with the married fathers than with the unmarried teachers. For some reason, they fascinate me more. I suppose if I were going to have an affair tomorrow, I'd select a married man, if only because he wouldn't be making time demands on me, like a single fellow would do. Also, married men probably are better for first-time lovers because they know better than to call when your husband's home and they don't get temperamental if you cancel a date because the Lord and Master wants to take you out that night."

Bev cheerfully admits that if everything continues as it has, she probably will become emotionally involved with other men, and maybe even sexually. But she would have to be deeply in love with a man before going to bed with him, and she doubts whether she could love another man and her husband simultaneously.

Which Comes First, Sex or Love?

Light-years apart from Bev is Myra, a thirty-four-year-old book illustrator. Her first marriage ended in divorce after three years and she lived alone for almost six years before marrying her current husband, a flight engineer for an airline. She has had affairs, a few very intense and several casual sexual adventures.

Myra's philosophy is that if she is strongly attracted to a man she tries to whisk him into bed at the first possible opportunity. She admits that this sounds much more casual than it really is, simply because she's highly selective and is not on the prowl.

"When I go to a restaurant, if I don't like the food I don't come back. Demanding love before sex is like reserving a table at the restaurant for a week straight without knowing whether the food is any good. If sexual attraction is strong, that part of a relationship should be undertaken as early as possible so both persons can look at one another objectively. When each one is panting to get into bed, he and she invariably cover up strong personality traits and try to behave as the other expects. Once the sexual ritual is out of the way, there is no need to posture or hide, and a person's real character bubbles to the surface.

"Another advantage to early sex is that it enables a woman to winnow out the men who are going to lean on her for mothering or who will become so dependent that the woman feels she mysteriously has become obliged to take care of them. These are the men who get very emotional in bed, men who cry a lot, men who emote about their sexual inadequacies. And that's another man I personally don't care to get tied up with—the guy who not only can't restrain himself sexually, but doesn't try. Sure, I feel sorry for him, but let him find some other woman to frustrate. If I get into bed with a man, it means that I'm excited as hell, just as I presume he is, and I expect to end up as satisfied as my partner. When this doesn't happen, I feel distinctly cheated."

Because Myra is an independent woman, what she does not get from her marriage she seeks elsewhere. Her husband does not provide the intense personal love that she sometimes wants, nor is he particularly imaginative in bed.

"When I got married the second time, I still didn't realize what a sexual animal I really was. I enjoyed the physical act of making love, but I had only experienced a real orgasm two or three times in my life. I guess that I was rather passive sexually when I remarried, probably because I really wanted George to turn me on."

Several years after her remarriage, she found herself strongly attracted to a single man, so she decided to see what he was like in bed. The results were a revelation to her, and she reports that she has subsequently experimented extensively with sexual infidelity. And with one of her partners she developed a strong emotional bond which is still there.

Hiding Affairs from Husbands

Myra perhaps is atypical in this respect, for her husband is away several days at a time, and she always knows his schedule. Also, she has no children and her profession requires her to travel to many cities to confer with art directors and editors about the books she is illustrating. The actual infidelities are no problem to hide, but she admits that occasionally the emotional or sexual side effects might be visible to a perceptive husband—"which George certainly is not!"

Wives with less freedom than Myra find that hiding infidelity is no great problem when married to men who are preoccupied with their jobs or their social activities. When confronted with a jealous, possessive husband, however, unfaithful wives have to fight hard to maintain a casual pose. The irony of this is that the more jealous and possessive the husband is, the less likely it is in the beginning that his wife is playing around. He storms and has tantrums when she comes home late from the bridge club, and his accusations slowly sink into her subconscious. If he keeps it up long enough, he ultimately will drive her into infidelity, if only because he has sung its praises so highly while berating her.

The Oral Contraceptives

A divorced man claims that the two greatest incentives to sexual freedom in recent years have been the development of oral contraceptives and pantyhose. "The Pill has done away with the last-minute rush to the bathroom to insert the diaphragm, and pantyhose have done away with the girdle, which so many women—especially married women—wear 'to keep up their stockings' but really as a chastity belt to deter half-hearted seducers. Now there is no reason for an interested woman not to climb into bed and enjoy sex fully."

The acreage of print devoted to arguments about whether the Pill is responsible for declining moral standards is as pointless as it is copious. The effect of oral contraceptives on married women has been extensive. Certainly they have given women a freedom from the clumsiness of diaphragms and the messiness of vaginal jellies and creams. The woman who was infidelity-prone before the oral contraceptives undoubtedly has found them to be marvelously uninhibiting. This woman, if she were married to a jealous or suspicious man, would have had to conduct contraceptive activities with outmost discretion. Some women report that their husbands have challenged them with having taken their diaphragms along with them because the husband couldn't find it in its customary place at home.

Another aspect of the oral contraceptive centers around wives who have enjoyed a stepped-up sex drive. As wives became aggressive sexually, the effect on their husbands' libidos sometimes was dramatic, causing the husband to retreat in terror. There is not much evidence to indicate that this reaction was widespread, but there were just enough reports to be significant.

The Pill and Promiscuity

Mildred is living proof for those who claim that the Pill unshackles sexual appetites and leads women into infidelity. Shortly after starting oral contraceptives, Mildred had a stormy affair with another married man, then followed it with an affair with a single man five years younger than she. What this story neglects to tell is the fact that Mildred was well on her way to infidelity before taking her first pill. She had been raised a Catholic with all the attending guilt feelings about contraceptives. After two children, however, she said to hell with the Church and had herself fitted with a diaphragm. Mildred at first had tried to persuade her husband Mike to use condoms so she wouldn't feel quite so sinful, but he refused on the grounds that condoms limited his sexual enjoyment. Also, Mike remained a strong Catholic as Mildred fell away from the Church, so he disapproved of her taking any precautions. Their sex life, as a result of the dissension between them over contraception, dwindled drastically. When the Pill became available, Mildred asked her doctor for a prescription. That night she nearly raped Mike, so delighted was she. Mike still wasn't sure about the theological implications of the Pill, but the outburst of sexuality from Mildred stunned him into impotence.

For the previous six months, Mildred had felt terribly disenchanted with her marriage. When they first met, Mike and Mildred were of comparable intelligence, but Mike had already reached the zenith of his growth while Mildred kept growing. As a result, six years later Mildred found herself married to an inferior man both intellectually and sexually. Mike had not really satisfied her in bed, except once or twice manually, and he deeply resented having to spend so much time on preliminaries.

Mildred thought about leaving Mike, but she felt no strong dislike for him. But she regretted marrying a man who had not continued to grow with her, and she became increasingly hostile toward his ineptness in bed.

When she started her first extramarital affair, she was looking for a man of comparable intelligence, someone she could spend time with. A girl friend suggested that Mildred join her at a folk-dancing club which attracted a number of interesting men. Mildred, like many others questioned for this book, found the first occasion for infidelity within a social or business group.

After two affairs, both of which developed from folk-dancing groups she regularly visits, Mildred has revised her attitude toward her marriage.

"I'll stay with Mike only as long as I have a reason to.

And God help him and this dreary marriage the moment an eligible, desirable man comes along."

Is she then hunting for a husband?

"Not necessarily. I want to find a man with whom I can develop a relationship that doesn't have to be based in marriage. Yes, I'd be willing to live with him if the love is strong enough and if he's able to support me properly."

Support?

"Of course. I intend to be self-sufficient as soon as the kids don't need baby-sitters, but until then I expect that the man I live with will support me."

The majority of wives surveyed about the effect of the Pill on their sex lives and marriages indicate that it might have a hastening influence, speeding someone along the road to infidelity or divorce, but that it was incapable of changing basic attitudes. Even the wife whose sexual appetite supposedly increases is usually just a woman whose appetite has been dampened by the discomfort or inconvenience of earlier forms of contraception.

Children and Domesticity

It is safe to generalize that the more intelligent and curious a wife is, the less happy she will be as a full-time mother and housekeeper. It is quite common in the business and professional worlds today to see wives get pregnant, take off three months or so to be delivered and then return to work, leaving the baby with a relative or nurse.

Such a woman will have little difficulty experimenting with infidelity, simply because she has not let her family or domestic duties interfere with her personal freedom. The woman who has stayed home with children for several years, however, may find it difficult at first, but for her the clubs and community groups often provide the first whiff of independence, a heady fragrance to many women.

The Bored Wife

Boredom in this instance refers to marital boredom rather than boredom with the drudgery of motherhood and housekeeping. A wife can be happy with her children and house but find her husband a crashing bore personally, emotionally, intellectually, conversationally, and sexually.

"Husbands are flat tires," is a statement by a successful seducer of married women that most unfaithful wives subscribe to.

"Frank is such a stick-in-the-mud. He never wants to go anywhere with me."

"I prefer it when Marty stays home because he's like an albatross around my neck. He doesn't like my friends and he won't hide his boredom."

"Robert is a prematurely old man, a thirty-five-year-old windbag. I know lawyers are long-winded, but my husband never shuts up and what he talks about is insufferably dull."

"Express an opinion on any subject you can think of and Harry will argue with you. God, why can't that man ever get off the debating rostrum?"

"Dennis makes love with the same enthusiasm he has for visiting my parents: It's something to do before falling asleep."

Why do American men marry, their wives ask in rebellion against hours and days and years of living with an opinionated mass of flesh that watches television, reads lots of newspapers, indulges in childish hobbies, and otherwise behaves like an unimaginative oaf.

This is the question of wives who are bored by their

marriages. There are many wives who react in the opposite way, bitching at their creative or compulsive husbands to slow down and behave like a typical American husband and father. And there even are wives whose temperament and interests are matched by their husbands, yet who experience a sense of boredom because there is no friction, no disagreement.

Single or Married Men?

This question is articulated only by those wives who have made up their minds to deliberately look outside of their marriages for satisfaction. The wife who drifts into infidelity may have already resolved the problem subconsciously.

Janine, twenty-nine, is a methodical wife who approached the subject clinically.

"When I realized that my marriage was, at best, adequate, I knew instinctively that I'd be turning to other men for companionship and affection. I had heard hair-raising stories about wives who get involved with married men, just as one of my closest friends told me how awful it was to have an affair with a single man. So I mentally noted the advantages and disadvantages of both groups of men as they would involve me, not anyone else.

"The disadvantages of being involved with a married man are that the involvement—presumably starting as a friendship, then maturing to a closeness—would never be able to progress past a certain point. If I were to become so attached to a married man, I'd find every way possible to spend as much time with him as I could, but I wouldn't be able to count on his doing the same.

"The disadvantage of the single man is just the opposite: He's too free, and as such would be expecting me to be available all the time. With a single man, I'd be the one who would be able to go only so far emotionally."

Despite her methodical approach, Janine has not yet had a serious extramarital affair. She did go to bed twice with an old boyfriend who moved into the neighborhood with his wife, but she doesn't count that. There are two men with whom she works who are candidates for a closer friendship, but Janine is not pursuing them yet.

The Pursuit of Younger Men

There are some women for whom the twinges of infidelity do not become sharp pangs until they have passed their youthful years. The saddest examples are the stereotyped matrons married to wealthy men and living in popular retirement resorts. These wives, some of them still attractive but many more of them anxious to taste the joys of sexual and personal fulfillment which their husbands cannot or will not give them, turn to younger men. Their attempts to seduce young men, even to the point of paying for their attentions, are sad and sometimes tragic.

More in the scope of this study are those wives who, from their late thirties on, turn to younger men for emotional satisfaction. These affairs do not carry the taint of the Miami Beach gigolo scene, for they often are genuine affairs conducted with passion or even love. That they happen with such frequency is due both to the attraction of certain women to younger men and that of young men to older women. Unfaithful husbands, usually those in their twenties, often claim that the older married woman is the best target, since she is easy to get into bed and does not require excessive seduction. "They don't yell, they don't swell, and they're grateful as hell," is a popular adage among these men.

For both persons, such affairs can be very pleasant. The

young man may be looking for an experienced woman who might teach him something new in bed. And the older woman is looking for the physical vitality and passion so missing in her own marriage. Even if she has engaged in a number of affairs with men her own age or older, she may be tempted to sample a hot, panting youngster. And they have a goodly supply to select from: Delivery boys, messengers, clerks, waiters, students working at summer resorts, struggling young married men who are artists, writers, poets, or playwrights.

When I was thirteen years old I worked as delivery-boy-clerk at a local drugstore. I met a variety of unusual creatures, ranging from lushes and addicts to astrologers and lecherous old homosexuals. Some engaged me in conversation, and most of them gave me reasonable tips. However, one extremely wet and windy night, the young pharmacist gave me a package to take over to a local divorcée on my way home.

"And make sure you don't let her take it out in trade," he called to me on my way out the door. Throughout the long walk to her apartment, I entertained wild visions of orgies and lurid erotic initiations. When I knocked on the door, the woman who answered it was wearing a housecoat over her nightgown. With one glance she sized me up, then invited me inside to wait while she got the money to pay for the package—which I later was told contained vaginal jelly. As I stood waiting for her, I glanced at the mirror in her living room and saw in it the reflection of another delivery boy from the drugstore, an inordinately handsome but shy fellow three years my senior.

He didn't notice me because he was very carefully nursing a can of beer. What struck me was that he was without a shirt. After the woman had dismissed me with the correct amount for the package plus a dime tip (even in 1950 that seemed somewhat stingy), I walked home in the rain fantasying about how to get an older woman into bed. The first thing to do on arriving at her apartment was to ask for a beer, then, while she was out getting it, whip off your shirt and wait for her reaction. It wasn't quite clear what precisely the woman would then do, but my imagination filled in the gaps.

This example is simply an illustration of how easy it is for a woman to obtain younger men if she wishes. Most married women interviewed for this book had interests several cuts higher than thirteen-year-old delivery boys from the local drugstore. Some resort to the neighborhood bar, where there usually are a variety of married men eager to make it extramaritally. Those women who followed this route maintain almost unanimously that while they can find sexual gratification in the neighborhood bar or the local swingers' pub, it is so transient that they are grossly disappointed.

Some women in the major metropolitan areas described their experiences in the pick-up bars. Marjorie, a forty-two-year-old mother of five, is separated from her husband, who continues to maintain a close watch over her social activities in the hope of catching her in a social indiscretion which would enable him to get custody of the children when the divorce action goes to the courts.

"A few months after Jack left, and once I realized the marriage was dead, a divorced girl friend suggested that we make the circuit of the 'single' bars in the nearby cities. We made a pact that we would arrive and leave together, to protect ourselves. Well, it was pretty stupid at first, with the young junior executives—with their goddamned attaché cases—dashing off with the stewardesses and secretaries—all carrying their overnight cases. Then one Friday night, when I was feeling particularly lonely, I tried to call Joyce but couldn't get her. So I hopped in the car and drove to a place we had visited frequently. (My mother was baby-sitting for me.) I must have sat at the table alone for at least an hour before this shy young man finally pulled himself away from the bar and asked me to have a drink with him. Of course, I was appropriately reluctant, but soon we were sitting next to each other as he was pouring out his line. Several drinks later, I suggested that he stop trying to ply me with liquor and speak openly. He was so embarrassed that I wanted to blush for him. We left the bar and drove to his apartment a few miles away, where everything became much more relaxed and certainly less strained. I told him to stop trying so hard and be himself. He told me about his divorce, which was quite messy, and I told him a bit about myself. I think he was resigned to a chatty evening at home with no sex until I pulled him down to me for a friendly kiss. That really got him steamed up, and he became so passionate that I started to respond. Well, I spent the night at his apartment, much to the annoyance of my mother, who didn't know what was going on and grumbled at having to stay all night with the children.

"I must say that Ralph was a good lover. He made me feel needed and wanted, and he also satisfied me physically as I never have been satisfied. When he realized that he actually was getting me into bed, his incredulity was so sweet. Apparently he hadn't had much luck at the singles bars, and he expected to be rebuffed at the last minute. I had to reassure him that I wanted to make love to him. I was totally without contraceptive precautions, but he had a large supply of condoms, and we spent several nice hours together.

"I haven't seen Ralph since then—which was two weeks ago—but he has called me several times. I have been back to the pick-up bars, perhaps because I've been looking for something a bit more meaningful than Ralph, but I haven't found it. Twice I've gone to bed with young men-on-the-make, and both times I've gotten the hell out of their apartments and driven back home with a certain sense of disgust at having been used.

"But I must admit that I enjoyed Ralph and I think I'll schedule a return date with him soon. I don't want to get married again, but having a younger man who is sexually and physically so active appeals to me. I don't know what I'll do when I become physically old, but I hope to God I'll have been able to find a good man to marry and to love for those years."

A different experience with the pick-up bars is cited by Sandra, a twenty-nine-year-old married woman.

"I don't want to be plied with liquor, taken across the street to a bachelor pad, quickly screwed, and then dumped into the street. If I go to bed, I want it to be with a man I have known at least long enough to like and respect. Sure I went the route of the pick-up bars, and I have had my fill of quickie sex.

"I cannot stand the thought that because I have grappled with a man for a few minutes in his bed, I should immediately become his worshipful mistress. The men I have met in the singles bars are rotten lovers and should be branded on the forehead to warn other women. Sure I was attracted to them, and sure I went to their apartments and went to bed with them, but going to bed with a man does not make him an expert lover. I think each man should be rated by the women he has screwed so that subsequent partners can evaluate his performance before deciding whether or not to go to bed with him."

"In the singles bars, every man between the ages of twenty-one and sixty is looking for a quick bedmate. Every woman between the same ages is looking for a meaningful relationship. To see this difference in action, visit a singles bar."

This is the view of a twenty-five-year-old single man, supported by the affirmation of many married, separated, and divorced men and women. The singles bar is one of the most depressing places to hunt for future partners, perhaps because of the necessity to lay it on the line. The man wants sex first and then he'll discuss the possibilities of a relationship. The woman is interested in getting such a relationship started before going to bed with the man. And yet both roles reverse at the singles bar. The man tries to imply that he is looking for a meaningful relationship while the woman implies that she is willing to jump into a passionate sexual embrace with the man.

Men at singles bars really are looking for a meaningful relationship just as much as single women want a robust sexual experience. The stereotypes are way off, but each sex continues to subscribe to them. Therefore, women continue to giggle, "Oh, you men are just interested in one thing," while men mutter, "Don't try to trap me into marriage."

Dissatisfied Wives

One comment often made by unfaithful wives was that they individually had abolished the double standard and preferred to regard infidelity the way men do—as something to be indulged in for whatever reason pleases them.

"Men can play around or get seriously involved without anyone telling them that they must be ready to leave their marriages before they can have an affair. That's what women have been told for hundreds of years and I say that's a lot of hot male air!" This was the reaction of Annie, a thirty-seven-year-old biologist who had been lectured by one of her fellow workers on why wives should not play around extramaritally. Annie, a stunningly attractive redhead even in her shapeless lab coat, admits to having five times the sex drive of her husband, Herb. Also, she describes him as a tranquil man who is very comfortable with Annie and makes few emotional demands on her. But Annie is highly charged with emotional needs and energy, and for years was very nervous from frustration.

"A dear friend of mine diagnosed my problem as resulting from dissatisfaction in marriage. My friend had suffered similarly until she had an affair. Her marriage ultimately ended in divorce because it was rotten to begin with. I've had several affairs since that conversation, and I'm still pleasantly married. Herb is really a sweet man so I stay married to him while filling my needs away from home. Herb may even suspect what I'm up to, for just the other night he hinted that he did not disapprove. What floored me was his implication that he might just do the same thing! For several years I've been looking at this marriage only from my own frustrated point of view. It never occurred to me that Herb might be dissatisfied."

The overwhelming conclusion one can draw about unfaithful wives is that, like husbands, they're looking for emotional and psychological fulfillment just as much as sexual gratification. Just as men defy their stereotype of looking only for sex, women often enter affairs primarily for sex, thus destroying the stereotype of the woman looking for love above all else.

> Man's love is of man's life a thing apart,
> 'tis woman's whole existence.

This was written by Lord Byron in the early years of the nineteenth century. An accomplished seducer and a brilliant coiner of poetic phrases, Byron today would be hooted at by most of the married women who were interviewed for this book. It's not that women have changed since Byron's era, but rather that men are getting a better look at them now that women no longer need to disguise their feelings and are relatively free to look around outside their marriages whenever they want.

There are, of course, thousands of women who describe themselves as perfectly happy in their marriages, or more realistically, they say that even if complete happiness is not always present they feel restricted by religious or moral inhibitions against any physical infidelity.

Curiosity, rebelliousness, and independence seem to go hand in hand in determining whether a married woman will experiment with one or more forms of infidelity.

Chapter Four

THE PRACTICAL STRATEGY OF INFIDELITY

> "My place or yours?"
> Ancient folk saying

Even when two people embark on an affair with a minimum of emotional conflicts, scruples, and moral inhibitions, the strategy of where and when to get together privately can tax the ingenuity of a field marshal. A close friendship that is only psychological and not yet at the emotional or sexual state can present problems where just being seen together might cause trouble for the pair. And when a couple is in love or having a hot sexual affair, privacy and intimacy are essential.

There are only a few variations on the basic situations of infidelity. When both partners are married they either sneak to one's house when the spouse is away or else they find some neutral meeting place. If a couple having an affair live in a small community, they often must meet in a different town or city.

Dangers of Extramarital Affairs

The chief fear of most unfaithful husbands and wives is that they will be caught and that their infidelity will become known to their mates. Because many practitioners of infidelity do *not* want to break up their marriages, they are afraid that an unhappy mate might well throw them out on grounds of adultery, even if there has been no sexual contact whatever. The married man who is seeing another woman knows that if his wife finds out about it, she may not divorce him but will make his life miserable. And the husband who has been cuckolded can be extremely vindictive toward his wife, even physically violent.

Where a marriage is already in trouble, the person who is engaging in infidelity cannot risk giving the mate ammunition that might be used in court to influence alimony payments or custody of the children.

Keeping the Affair in the Community

Despite the advice of experts in infidelity, both male and female, many husbands and wives insist on conducting affairs in their own communities. There are some men and women who don't give a damn whether or not the neighbors see the affair. John Updike's *Couples* offers an excellent description of such people, although he perhaps has condensed too much open infidelity into such a small community. However, the majority of individuals interviewed about infidelity indicated a strong desire to keep their neighbors and their spouses in the dark.

When people do practise infidelity in their own communities, it is when one of the partner's husband or wife is out of town or travels frequently or is visiting relatives in another state. This gives them a meeting and bedding place, assuming of course there are no complications with children.

Infidelity at Home

When an affair is conducted in one of the partner's homes, a host of tricky questions and problems arise. The most comonly reported concern where to make love and which contraceptives to use (assuming the woman is not taking the Pill). Men and women report an aversion on the part of many to making love in their own marital bed or even on the marital couch.

"I wouldn't think of insulting my husband by letting a man into our bed. We used one of the children's beds instead."

"I'd really feel like a louse to make love to a woman in my wife's bed. Well, sure, it's my bed too, but think of how she'd feel if she found out. We did it on the living-room rug."

"Christ, Betty can't stand her husband and he's gone so much that they're virtually separated, but she refuses to let me cuckold him doubly by taking her in their bed. I don't want to cuckold her husband—I want to make love to Betty and I don't care where we do it."

Since contraception is such an intimate aspect of marriage, the person who is having an affair often prefers not to use anything from the home supply. This is awkward when a woman uses a diaphragm, for she then has to get fitted for another or rely on vaginal foam. She can also try to coax her partner into using condoms—which happens a surprisingly high percentage of the time. Those women who are not overly happy at home or who have no moral or religious inhibitions just bring their diaphragms from home when meeting a man.

Some unfaithful women are so relaxed and unrestricted by conventional morality that they even will use contraceptive jellies or foams belonging to their partner's wife.

Martha is such a wife. She lives in a large city and works as a bookkeeper. During her affair with Rick, they would alternate apartments. Both were married to partners who were gone from home for regular periods of time.

"One time we were at Rick's and I had forgotten to bring my diaphragm and I couldn't go back to get it because my husband was home. It was Sunday afternoon and there weren't any drugstores open so I asked Rick where his wife kept her foam. Rick asked if I would let him use one of my husband's rubbers sometime and I said sure. However, I've thought about it and my dear husband is such a cheap bastard that he probably counts them and might notice one missing. Besides, I don't care for them. Some women don't seem to mind but they're just not much fun."

Whenever possible, a married person having an affair prefers it to be where both persons can relax and not fear surprise or detection. If one of the partners lives alone, that settles the problem. When both are married, however, and neither wants to entertain the partner at home, the only recourse is a neutral meeting place, such as a hotel or motel.

The Hotel-Motel Guilt

Married persons tend to balk at checking into a motel or hotel for a one-night stay. This is particularly true in the beginning of an affair when the act of checking into a room in one's home community is an open admission that both expect to make love.

Several married women report that they initially resisted motels and hotels because of guilt about openly admitting what they knew and wanted. As the affair progressed, and as they became more experienced, this guilt disappeared.

Another reason for this reluctance is that the couple usually checks in under a phony name and address. At least one piece of luggage is necessary to fool the hotel personnel (who rarely are fooled but who don't give a damn). When a motel is used, no luggage is necessary since the car is driven directly to the front door of the room and the registration desk is bypassed.

Some couples get around the deceitful aspects of hotel-motel rooms by having just the man check into a single room and then smuggling the woman in a little later. In large hotels in big cities this is quite easy, but in a small hotel it is frowned upon by the management, who view the practise not as immoral but as unethical in that it deprives the hotel of the extra money that would be charged for the second person.

This single-room technique works well in most motels, also. The more adept married men favor this technique where there are many motels to choose from.

When the partners live in small communities, they are virtually forced into motels, which can be found almost everywhere in the United States.

The initial aversion to hotels and motels on the part of some men and women does not hold true if the place is in a distant city. When both partners are staying at a hotel on a business trip out of town, the reluctance vanishes.

Apartment Borrowing

When hotels and motels are not practical or they are unattractive, the clever practitioner of infidelity usually will discover a single friend who is willing to let the couple use his apartment on occasion. Whether this works effectively depends to a large extent on how relaxed and self-confident the woman is, and whether she minds sharing her romantic secret with her lover's friend. This apartment borrowing is rather common in large cities. A man and a woman who each have many friends in the city will have a wide variety of trysting places to choose from, and they can change locations regularly so as not to wear out their welcome.

Some friendships have been severely strained by thoughtless lovers who took advantage of a borrowed apartment to snoop, drink up the liquor supply, leave a batch of dirty dishes in the sink, spill ashes on the carpet, fail to put away phonograph records, and—worst of all—stain the bed linen and leave a neatly-made bed mussed.

Julie doesn't really belong in this book, because she's never been married or even slept with a married man. However, she did lend her apartment to Liz who worked with her in computer programming. Liz was having a red-hot affair with Bill, an engineer in a neighboring department of the same company. Bill was married and Liz lived at home with her parents, one of whom was always there. Julie was very fond of Liz and even though she didn't think much of Bill, she gave Liz the key for a weekend when she was going to visit her family.

Julie came straight back to work Monday morning without stopping at her apartment. Liz almost immediately dragged her off to the ladies' room to tell her what a marvelous weekend they had. Liz didn't go into clinical details but she assured Julie that Bill was a good lover. Later that day, she met Bill as they both were leaving the cafeteria. He nudged her with his elbow and winked conspiratorially at her. They were walking with several friends when Bill turned to her.

"Julie, I'll bet you've got more black underwear than any other single girl in this city. Don't you ever wear anything except black nylon?"

Julie was shocked, not so much at his loud words in front of friends, but at his brazen admission of going through her dresser. However, she turned to him and raised her voice loud enough for everyone to hear.

"Sure Bill, but I always hide my other colors when I'm having friends over to snoop. Did you have a nice weekend with your girl friend?"

It took Julie three hours Monday night to straighten up and clean her apartment. Furniture had been moved, dishes put away in the wrong cabinet, and ashtrays filled (but not emptied) all over the house. What most infuriated her was not the mess, but the visible evidence that Bill had gone through the entire apartment. Fortunately, she kept all personal correspondence and confidential papers locked in a strongbox.

Bill demonstrated his excellent taste by drinking her full bottle of Chivas Regal and leaving the empty on the dresser in the bedroom. Julie also learned a few weeks later that he had used her phone to call his wife twice, and he put three other toll calls on her bill.

"I wanted to throw the bill under his nose in front of everyone else in his department, and then tell them what a cheap son of a bitch he really was," Julie said bitterly. "I even thought of calling his wife anonymously and giving her the essential details, but I decided that might hurt her more than it would him. Needless to say, that was the last time I've let anyone borrow my apartment."

THE GREAT OUTDOORS

The woods are traditionally the place for a quick sexual bout, and some lovers are inclined to try an outdoor session if the weather is nice and if they can't find anywhere else to be alone. The idea of making love in a sylvan setting, two bodies rolling on the earth with leaves and flowers in the hair is certainly romantic. But it overlooks two invariables: insects and *homo sapiens*. A swarm of mosquitoes, flies, ticks, or gnats can route even the most turned-on couple. And unless the lovers disappear into the remotest forest—which is not likely for an afternoon session—they cannot avoid man or his debris. The loveliest copse may be suited for love, but chances are good that it often has been used for precisely that and visible mementoes of previous amours will be sprinkled about. A conservationist who also practises infidelity estimates that it would take him two days of hiking away from the roads to find a lovemaking spot that was not already studded with beer cans, broken bottles, and other traces of man's occupancy.

Couples who have tried outdoor lovemaking point out that even if the bugs are not fierce and the litter isn't overpowering, there is a distinct possibility of a Boy Scout patrol hiking past.

Getting Out of the House

Married persons who are ready for infidelity usually have little difficulty getting out of the house for evenings or days. When both are married, they respect each other's obligations to get back home by a reasonable hour. When one of the partners is single, this nightly departure can become highly traumatic; it has been blamed specifically for the breakdown of many affairs.

A married woman often can get free at night without much sweat, particularly if she has made her husband feel guilty about cooping her up at home all day and being too tired to entertain her at night—a familiar procedure for wives who want to control their husbands. The guilt-ridden male will agree to anything to get the source of guilt off his back. These women have their evenings filled with activities and functions so that they can arrange to be gone several nights each week without stirring a whisker of a doubt on the chin of the man in front of the television set. She has her tennis lessons, art class, the drama club, the bowling league, yoga lessons, and all the social and religious clubs.

Although it is possible to conduct a quickie affair for a few hours at a time a few nights a week, both partners rarely like that and connive to spend more time together. One way is for the married woman to hurry out of the house as soon as her husband comes home from work, meet her lover, and adjourn either to a bar (if the affair is still in the emotional, talking stages) or to bed. She then can stay out quite late if she has already conditioned her husband to expect her home late. If she hasn't, he may become suspicious and start questioning her closely.

If she lives in a big city or in a large suburban area, she also can use the late shopping hours certain nights of the week as an excuse for not being home to prepare supper. That way she can meet her lover early in the afternoon and they can stay together for several hours.

The married man can always arrange to work late at his job, or to moonlight by holding down a night job, or comfort a close friend who is in trouble with his wife, or any number of imaginative excuses.

To Be Seen or Not to Be Seen

Most married persons who are unfaithful do not want their spouses to learn about it, often out of a genuine desire not to hurt them. Several of those interviewed regard infidelity as therapeutic for their marriages, releasing pressures that otherwise would build to an intolerable degree.

A man and woman who work together and are close friends can eat lunch together and go out after work for a drink with no comment. But the moment they begin to have an affair, they radiate signals that certain other individuals seem to be able to pick up on a psychic radar. Even though they try hard to disguise the deepening intensity of their feelings, two people in love or even just interested in one another will rapidly be detected unless they go through an elaborate charade of hardly recognizing one another. But even then, the first time a mutual friend spots them walking down the street arm-in-arm or sitting close together in a restaurant or cocktail lounge, their masquerade will be penetrated.

The simplest solution is for them to continue to behave like friends and then deny any hints or innuendos with a smile. A pleasant denial that does not attempt to register shock and outrage at such a suggestion often will disarm the most suspicious person.

There are men who, in office romances, will respond to an accusation with a wistful smile and a remark such as:

"Boy, I sure would like to with her! She's a real honey, isn't she? But she's really having a hard time right now with some guy she's really hung up on. Anybody who fools around with her won't get very far, I bet."

If the we're-just-good-friends approach is used correctly, it's very difficult to be caught in a compromising situation, unless, of course, one of the spouses hires a private detective to take pictures of the couple in bed together.

Some husbands and wives who plan to find companionship or gratification from within the company or social organization, will practise preventive maintenance by making sure that their mates meet all their friends, including prospective lovers. If carefully handled, this maneuver can effectively anesthetize the spouse so that whenever he or she hears the lover's name it is dismissed as just another friend who is constantly being chattered about.

When this step has been taken and the spouse actually knows the lover, then it is possible for the two lovers to move around together with some impunity. If any nasty gossip trickles back to the mate, it can always be blamed on the vicious tongue or vivid imagination of the gossiper.

INCRIMINATING EVIDENCE

Men and women who have become accomplished practitioners of infidelity are very hesitant to get involved with neophytes who are prone to carelessness and forgetfulness. While some experienced persons may go to elaborate lengths to destroy all incriminating evidence, the effect of experience generally is to provide the person with an instinctive check list of what to look for, what to destroy, and whether the partner is effectively covering his or her tracks.

People who practise infidelity, particularly the sexual phase, usually will have enough sense to check for lipstick marks, powder smudges, telltale stains, etc., but they often will carry home slips of paper with telephone numbers, addresses, or short notes on them—all of which can be sifted through by a suspicious husband or wife.

Most affairs are accompanied by a wining and dining phase near the beginning, often exercising a drain on the budget that can become noticeable to a man's wife or a woman's husband. When lovers exchange gifts, as is their wont, the married ones need to think carefully about an explanation when they bring the gifts home.

And most incriminating of all are the mysterious telephone calls to the married partner's home. When the same voice comes on the phone regularly, a spouse is going to start wondering.

Getting rid of evidence is recommended by experienced lovers, particularly when the affair moves into a phase which may arouse the spouse's suspicions, causing him or her to start hunting for evidence. Unfortunately, many men and women cannot tell at what point active suspicion starts. Most of these individuals ultimately divorce, but a few remain in looser marriages.

Codes for Telephone Calls and Letters

Partners in an infidelity who are forced to use the telephone or the dubious services of the Post Office often resort to elaborate codes and cryptic messages. The dispassionate observer may be prompted to ask why such elaborate steps are taken when simple messages are so much easier. The answer is that many practitioners of infidelity seem dedicated to subterfuge. The more complicated the code, the happier they are. Most observers and catalogers of infidelity will agree that a strong streak of masochism often accompanies infidelity. Psychiatrists often claim that this is the result of guilt feelings, but it seems too pat an explanation.

Many married persons will warn members of the opposite sex in whom they are interested to be careful when telephoning them at home or writing to them in order to avoid arousing the suspicions of a jealous mate. John, a forty-two-year-old father of six regards himself as permanently married—at least until his children are in college or married. However, he frequently is embroiled in affairs of varying intensity with women who work for the same corporation. John is an attorney who holds an important executive position, one which gives him ready access to attractive, ambitious women who are not too important in the corporation to cramp his style. When John becomes involved with a woman, he often encourages her to call him at home. As the affair progresses, the codes for their conversation become more elaborate, so as not to make his wife suspicious. Once into an affair, John usually tells his wife that the girl who is calling is a special assistant assigned to work with him on a crash program, and therefore must call him frequently.

"My wife seems to accept these explanations, although she becomes suspicious the moment an unfamiliar female voice calls. When the girl is single and lives alone, there is no question about where the affair will develop. When she's married or lives with other people, then we have to confine it to business trips. I travel out of town at least twice a month, and it's not too hard to arrange for my friend to join me. When we only see each other intimately on these trips, we may talk over the phone several times a week, especially on weekends when we are isolated from one another.

"In my fourteen years with the company, I've had maybe nine major affairs and a half-dozen or more casual flings. Why do I keep it up? Quite simple. I need this diversion to keep me alert and interested in life. My job is really rather dull, but when I know that someone I love is standing near me, watching what I do with admiration, it gives me enthusiasm to do a better job. Also, before I ever started chasing other women, I was a terrible grouch around the house. I was constantly snapping at the kids or yelling at my wife. Now, I'm too preoccupied to be surly, and everyone loves me at home. Well, everyone except my wife, who thinks I'm a company husband.

"I've thought about divorce, but knowing my wife, she'd do her damnedest to get me fired from my job, and this I don't need. Maybe when the youngest is in college I'll move out.

"Whenever a woman calls me at home, I insist that she couch her comments in office terms. If she wants me to meet her at her apartment the next morning, she'll tell me I have an executive committee meeting at 10 A.M. This means that her roommate or husband will be gone by then and I can meet her. Or if we are meeting someplace else, the code changes accordingly.

"The reason for all this subterfuge is that I'm deathly afraid that my wife might pick up one of the extension phones in the house and hear some woman pouring out her heart to me. This I don't need."

When the Spouse Becomes Suspicious

Detected infidelity can present unpleasant problems to the person who is not looking for an excuse to get out of a marriage. In addition to boring conversation, it can produce fights, tantrums, and occasionally, divorce. Also, the married person who is successfully leading an active extramarital life risks increased domestic vigilance if infidelity is discovered.

Thus, one of the most important problems for the unfaithful person is to make sure that the spouse does not become suspicious or, if that does occur, to have a plausible excuse to accompany the denial. It is very easy to reassure the husband or wife who wants to believe that an unfaithful mate really is monogamous, just as it is next to impossible to convince the ultra-suspicious spouse of one's innocence.

Because each marriage is different, the methods of reassuring suspicious husbands and wives vary sufficiently to present a check list.

Robert, a twenty-nine-year-old editor, automatically starts to fabricate excuses and alibis when he is spending any significant amount of time with another woman. If he is just cruising after work among the girls who work for the same newspaper, he doesn't worry. But the moment he starts to pursue seriously, his wife seems to detect the difference and becomes suspicious. He reassures her by saying he has to work late, or must do some elaborate research at the library, or has gotten stuck at the last minute conducting an interview with some important person. When he is gone from the office during the day, he always covers his tracks by leaving word with his secretary that he will be in a meeting all afternoon.

Bernadette, a thirty-five-year-old advertising production manager, finds that her husband starts to act suspicious whenever he wants attention from her. She has had three or four affairs during their ten-year marriage, and she thinks he probably is aware of it. However, she goes out of her way to reassure him whenever he shows the least signs of restlessness. Her verbal approach usually soothes him, Bernadette reports.

Even when the unfaithful partner has no desire to preserve the marriage, he or she may reassure the spouse or deny infidelity simply to keep that admission of guilt out of the hands of a vindictive spouse, or worse, the spouse's lawyer, if the case moves into divorce court.

Excessive Emotional Involvement

Some newcomers to extramarital love affairs object to the word "excessive," since it implies a moral dividing line. Those married persons who have had a variety of intense relationships extramaritally, however, support the concept of excessive emotional involvement.

"A love affair is out of control when one or both persons can see each other only as part of a fantasy, when their real world is being denied, when self-delusion takes over." This is the definition of a thirty-eight-year-old woman. Curiously, it is almost word-for-word similar to the definition of a thirty-year-old man.

The majority of persons who have had intense extramarital affairs claim they have set guidelines for themselves and that they try to stick to them to avoid getting hurt. Despite their experience, these persons are not always successful.

Joanne is forty-one, on her second marriage, which she would like to keep healthy. Neither she nor her husband expects the other to be completely monogamous, but Joanne is afraid that an excessively emotional affair might seriously disrupt her marriage.

"I've been through two super-fantasy affairs where I was living in a dream. I crashed so hard after the first one that I promised myself never to get that deeply involved. Years later, I met a man who touched me profoundly and who, like me, was susceptible to emotional excesses. I won't describe the background, but it was just what I needed to rocket into love. And then, when everything I wanted wasn't right there waiting for me, I dipped into fantasy, as did he. Fortunately, we both started to come out of it at the same time, so there was no terrible crash and no horribly bruised psyches. We both felt very wistful that our love could only flourish in unreality. We still love each other, but very gently. Now when I am attracted to a man, and even when something starts to develop, I immediately throw the barbed wire around my emotions to keep him from getting too close and possibly even exciting me to the point of no return. I don't think it will happen to me again as long as I'm married to Roy. If we ever break up, or should he die, then I can't say that I won't permit myself to let go of my emotions."

All individuals interviewed for this study who had undergone extreme emotional involvement condemned it for their futures, insisting that they would shun it, but many of them look back on it nostalgically. Those who had been badly burned by the collapse of an unrealistic love affair often look back with bitterness, especially if the other partner was responsible for puncturing the happy-gas balloon. Bitterness also is seen when a fantasy affair disintegrates after it has broken up a marriage.

Bob and Michele both work for a film-production company. Bob is a thirty-five-year-old cameraman and Michelle, twenty-seven, is a production assistant. Both were married at the time they met, and each had children. Their affair was cataclysmic, raging at white heat for nearly six months (intense affairs tend to last for a shorter duration than the participants realize at the time). Everyone in the company knew about it, and it was not long before their respective mates suspected that something was going on. Michelle's husband became violently jealous, and made several scenes over the telephone as well as on location when Michelle was out with a camera crew. Bob's wife confined her rage to the home, screaming at him and threatening to divorce him. After a particularly unpleasant night, Bob packed a suitcase and moved out. A week later his wife sued for divorce, and he told his lawyer to accept any reasonable terms from her lawyer. Meanwhile, Michelle was demanding that her husband move out, but he adamantly refused, arguing that if she wanted a divorce she could bloody well pack up and leave. Her lawyer suggested several nasty tricks to get him out, but Michelle decided it would be easier to take the two children and move into an apartment in town. Their respective domestic crises had kept Bob and Michelle from spending as much time together as they had previously, and when both divorces seemed to be moving along smoothly, they discovered that the white-hot passion had cooled a bit. Both were shocked and disappointed, but Michelle blamed Bob for this while he withdrew into himself. She would berate him and pick at him, but Bob would quietly turn her off and disassociate himself during the tirades. One night he looked at her and realized he was getting from her exactly what had driven him away from his wife. They stopped seeing each other for several weeks, then tried to start again, but this attempt ended in failure. Both are bitter.

Emotional Blackmail

Whenever passion soars beyond the boundaries of emotional control, a partner in an affair runs the risk of blackmail. There is, of course, the obvious blackmail possibilities where one partner threatens to tattle to the other's spouse if a particular price is not paid. This price may be money, but more often it is power or self-improvement.

A common form of this emotional blackmail occurs when a married man gets involved with a woman who is beneath him in the occupational hierarchy but who wants to rise. He gets emotionally involved with her, and she then puts the screws to him to help her advance, regardless of whether she has merit or talent. Her method of blackmail may be as crude as threatening to tell his wife, but more often it is simply withholding herself, denying him sexual gratification, or throwing tantrums when he wants love. Sometimes this blackmail is so disguised by the woman that her partner convinces himself that he is taking her under his wing and personally guiding her career.

In certain occupational settings, notably show business, the emotional trappings have been stripped away and sex is used as wampum. A director who really wants a particular young lady may have to bargain with her and promise (or pretend to promise) to cast her in his next picture or next play. And the actress or singer who is convinced that she has talent but doesn't seem to be getting anywhere finds that sleeping with the right people can do wonders for her career.

The most painful blackmail is when no overt threats are made, but emotional strings are pulled tightly around the victim's psyche. Denial is the most common and the most deadly weapon in a wildly torrid love affair. Strong men can be brought to their knees and independent women reduced to begging.

Gossip

"The only infidelity that can be kept secret is that conducted out of town, on a one-time basis, with no subsequent emotional involvement, letters, or telephone calls," is the opinion of a thrice-married man who now regards himself as "protectively monogamous."

His point is that no matter how discreet two lovers may be, they rapidly give themselves away to their friends, fellow workers, or mates. Because infidelity is such a personal matter, many persons indulging for the first time in a serious affair feel the need to confide in a best friend. Or when a close friend confronts them with an accusation, they grin and acknowledge it, glad to be able to talk about it.

The moment this happens, or when casual friends observe a twosome that looks too close, gossip flies. A couple may think they are carrying on the ideal discreet affair yet be stunned one day by the discovery that most of their friends know about it.

It is the opinion of virtually every practitioner of infidelity that once gossip is rampant, the spouse will soon hear it. Enemies are certainly dangerous, but friends often make damaging hints and allusions. Friends shared by both husband and wife may feel sorry for the "wronged" partner and feel a moral obligation to call his or her attention to the mate's infidelity. The most notorious tattlers seem to be those friends who themselves have been engaging in extramarital affairs. And the worst possible source of gossip is the former lover who desires vengeance.

Joanie had a brief but tempestuous affair with Ed, but after they broke up, she became friendly with Ed's wife, Brenda. Ed remained fond of Joanie and saw her every day at the plant, as well as socially. When Ed found himself embroiled in a sticky affair with a woman who was pressuring him to get out of his marriage, he confided in Joanie. He described the intensity of his new affair and listened gratefully as Joanie offered him sympathetic advice.

What Ed did not realize was that Joanie had once hoped that he would leave his wife for her, and she now violently resented the fact that he was seriously thinking of doing just that for another woman. Joanie waited until she was alone with Brenda and steered the conversation around to Ed. Very subtly, she informed Brenda that Ed liked to play around and currently was involved with another woman.

Brenda knew that her ten-year-old marriage with Ed was at a critical point, but she had no clear evidence that he was playing around. Joanie very carefully made no mention of her own previous involvement with Ed, but rather told Brenda she was speaking as a close friend of both, a friend who wanted to save a good marriage.

The result of Joanie's interference was the immediate destruction of a marriage which might have survived. Brenda confronted Ed with Joanie's story, and he admitted it. Before he could work through the problem of whether to leave the marriage or fight to save it, Brenda filed for divorce. Two years after the divorce became final, both Brenda and Ed separately admitted that they had behaved foolishly. Ed remarried but that marriage lasted less than a year. He started to date Joanie and learned what she had done to his marriage. Almost melodramatically, he stopped seeing her and began to court Brenda again. They have talked about remarrying, but have not yet done so. Brenda has said that if they do, she will insist that they move to another city and establish a whole new group of friends. Ed claims that he really wants to be monogamous.

Chapter Five

THE SOCIAL-LEGAL JUNGLE OF INFIDELITY

The old bastions of monogamous morality—the Law and the Church—are crumbling. Roman Catholics divorce as easily as Protestants and Jews. New York State's ancient anti-adultery and divorce laws have been laughed into oblivion while California, a state that many Americans regard as the home of crackpots and reactionaries, has adopted the most enlightened divorce law in the nation. The word *divorce* does not even appear in the revised California law. Instead, it provides for *dissolution* of a marriage on only two grounds: insanity and irreconcilable differences. In other words, if a married couple cannot live harmoniously together, they need not fish through the legal grab bag for phrases such as *mental cruelty, desertion, adultery,* or even *incompatibility.* Property is divided equally, and child custody is awarded on the basis of which partner can best care for the child. If the children are awarded to the wife, the husband is expected to support them. However, alimony is only provided where a wife is unable to support herself because she has to raise young children.

As divorce becomes simpler, abortion laws are easing. It no longer is necessary for a pregnant woman to seek out an abortion mill in the city or fly to Puerto Rico or London for an abortion.

Contraception is no longer an embarrassing conversation with the pharmacist but an unashamed prescription for the Pill, a fitted diaphragm, or an intrauterine device. When testimony before a Congressional committee about possible dangers from oral contraceptives frightened many women, manufacturers of condoms immediately jumped into the advertising gap with ads about the absence of side effects associated with their products. Druggists were supplied with counter displays of condoms which they were supposed to bring out to convince bashful husbands who were uncertain about which condom to purchase. But many druggists simply placed the display rack on the counter and, to their surprise, almost as many women as men purchased condoms.

Until the sudden adverse publicity about the Pill, many men regarded condoms as aesthetically repulsive. However, the introduction of a new line featuring a "dry lubricant" won converts when husbands discovered that they could use condoms with almost no loss of sensation.

Even premarital sex has become liberated. Physicians prescribe the Pill for teen-agers, and many parents philosophically accept the fact that their daughters are determined to prevent unwanted pregnancies. Boys and girls living together openly are common in college communities, and even conservative parents discover that their children, when away from home for the first time at college, almost feel compelled to defy them in the most brazen way imaginable—engaging in premarital sex. Where parental prejudice is rather strong, the defiant child may elect to have an affair with a member of a different race, nationality, or religion.

These are the advances over traditional morality that

have been achieved in modern times. Abortion, divorce, contraception, and premarital sex have established themselves so strongly that legal action against them would be inadvisable. Only extramarital sex—part of the complex of emotions and behaviors which we call *infidelity*—remains to be liberated. Even homosexuality between consenting adults is winning some support, but infidelity still is roundly condemned. And infidelity—or at least adultery—is illegal in almost every state, under laws stemming from the naïve innocence of our pious predecessors who insisted that their morality be legislated for everyone else. The Ten Commandments, a rustic moral code of a nomadic tribe, inveighs against adultery, listing it in the thundering thou-shalt-not column.

Not only is adultery legislated against, but American laws traditionally have made divorce a prolonged, nasty business. While grumblingly conceding that divorce may be a necessity, the moralists and legislators have recognized that where divorce is forbidden, prostitution flourishes. In many Catholic countries, where divorce is legally unobtainable, married men and women find emotional satisfaction in extramarital affairs, while those men looking for quick sexual satisfaction can find it with a prostitute who is licensed, medically-examined, and otherwise certified—if not blessed—by the church-controlled state.

One curious by-product of the rise of infidelity and divorce is the decline of the old-fashioned whorehouse. Once a thriving institution in every city of the United States, Europe, and Asia, the whorehouse now survives only in the rattier seaport cities of America.

Infidelity Among the Wealthy

Infidelity often has been an unspoken family tradition among the wealthy, particularly as a protection against divorce and the extensive publicity that might surround it. During the twentieth century there have been numerous wealthy men and women who have migrated through many marriages, with each divorce earning considerable newspaper and magazine space, especially when it is surrounded by lurid details of domestic squabbling and infidelities.

However, the quietly wealthy or famous seem capable of adjusting to the code that permits discreet infidelity when a marriage becomes dull or sour. It is almost a truism that when there is enough money in the bank account, acceptable infidelity can hold together the shakiest marriage, providing that each partner wants to avoid divorce.

Unwritten Rules for Infidelity

Whether they be rich or not-so-rich, couples tend to subscribe to a handful of unwritten rules in order to sanction infidelity while preserving marriage. The first of these is never to humiliate the spouse publicly by flaunting the affair. The husband who parades his lover before his wife is as socially reprehensible as the wife who brazenly cuckolds her husband and does not make any effort to hide it from him. This rule is applicable throughout society, and its violation can lead to ostracism. This is not to say that a married person who breaks this rule will immediately lose every close friend. Rather, the friends frequently will divide, some siding with the unfaithful partner while others support the spouse.

Jan, the thirty-seven-year-old wife of a lawyer, became openly involved in an affair with a thirty-one-year-old novelist, Bert. Jan and her husband were socially very active and when her affair became known, Jan discovered that she really didn't have that many friends. She made the socially-gauche error of bringing Bert to a cocktail party, then carrying on with him in front of her friends. The two of them sat on a couch, nuzzling and kissing, whispering to each other, obviously seriously involved. The hostess knew about Jan's affair, but she was shocked that it was being paraded out in the open. Several persons at the party were good friends of Jan's husband and they were upset that Jan wasn't more discreet. As the affair developed, Jan's husband learned about it and a rift opened between them. However, neither wanted a divorce. The marital relationship remained strained for almost four months, until Jan and Bert broke up and Jan told her husband that everything was over and that she would try to make their marriage work. During that time, however, Jan found that several couples who had been friendly with them cut her off coldly while still remaining friendly with her husband. The only friends she retained were those unmarried ones who had known her and liked her as a person and not as part of a couple.

Another unwritten rule is that a married person having an affair must shun publicity and keep the children innocent of the affair. The man or woman who is tickled at being gossiped about often is regarded as a fool.

"If Lorraine is so willing to let the rest of the world know that she is having an affair with someone, she might just be stupid enough to blab about some of my indiscretions. That's why I have cut her completely out of my social circle." This is the view of a tolerant but prudent publishing executive about his wife.

Bickering couples who drag children into the mess of an affair may find themselves ostracized by their friends for not handling their problems in a less conspicuous manner. There is something socially repugnant about children being subjected to the vicious battles between parents over infidelity. No matter how guilty of the same offense they may have been themselves, friends of a feuding couple become righteous over such exposure of children. What is even worse is when children are forced to choose between battling parents, or when they are called upon as witnesses to the profligate behavior of a mother or father.

Society has a strange way of ostracizing some divorced individuals while accepting others. A man who thought several couples were especially friendly toward him may find that they only accepted him as half of a marriage. Generally, individual friendships will survive a divorce while friendships between couples will divide and go to one partner or the other or neither.

Chapter Six

PERMISSIVE INFIDELITY

Permissive infidelity is nothing more than an agreement, tacit or open, between a husband and wife that either or both may engage in varying degrees of infidelity with no unpleasantness about it. Permissive infidelity may be as old as monogamy but only in recent years has it been recognized and accepted by some married couples. It ranges from the extreme of open mate-swapping to the more common practise of not asking questions when a husband or wife seems to be involved with someone else.

Some couples use permissive infidelity as preventive maintenance to keep a good marriage from becoming dull or stale. Others resort to it after the boredom already has set in. It sometimes is used as a last-ditch attempt to salvage a doomed marriage.

Permissive infidelity is rarely seen among the morally inhibited, at least not during their first marriages. Occasionally it develops in subsequent marriages among the nine-to-fivers, the steady jobholders who live in the suburbs and may not possess a curious or creative temperament. But the restless individual is a much more likely candidate for permissive infidelity, if only because he or she knows from experience that no one human being can be all things to another.

The popular conception of permissive infidelity is mate-swapping, a phenomenon that seems to exist lividly in men's imaginations but actually is quite rare. The reason for its rarity is the difficulty of assembling two or more couples who all are eager to exchange partners for a night or more. A fast reading of the ads in some of the racier tabloids provides an image of desperate middle-aged couples, hungry to discover similar-minded couples with whom they can exchange Polaroid photographs and arrange to meet for an orgy.

It is impossible to estimate accurately the amount of such mate-swapping that goes on in the United States, but evidence indicates that there is only a small percentage of formal interchanging of partners.

An interesting example of mutual permissive infidelity was seen in the case of Ralph and Susan (Chapter One). They have a tacit agreement that permits either to occasionally spend time away from home without having to undergo intensive cross-examination upon return. Both Ralph and Susan believe that this freedom has enhanced their marriage, but they recommend it only for those couples whose marriages are strong.

Ralph and Susan cannot be considered typical of permissive infidelity, because each not only consents to the other's activities, but seems at least vaguely aware of what is going on.

Cathy and Karl are probably more typical in that while each feels free to spend time with other partners, each also goes to pains to disguise the affair and to pretend not to see what the other is doing.

"I suppose we might someday drag the whole business out in the open," Karl predicts. "It probably would be healthier if we admitted that we know what is going on, but I really prefer it this way. I know Cathy plays occasionally, but I don't want to know with whom and how. I'm willing to look the other way and pretend not to notice what's going on. If I acknowledged that she was involved with another man, then curiosity might force me to ask her about him, and pretty soon I'd be asking about what they did together, whether she went to bed with him, and if so, how he compares as a lover with me. And damn it, I don't want to know those answers. If I happened to know the guy Cathy was involved with, I might think poorly of her taste if he was a jerk. Or I might tear myself to pieces wondering why I wasn't enough for her. No, I don't want to know any details, thank you! I suspect that Cathy occasionally has a fling, and that's all I want to know. This works nicely in reverse, too, for when I spend the night with an old girl friend or one of my friends at work, I carefully disguise it so Cathy doesn't get suspicious. Oh she probably knows, but I'm damned if I'll rub her nose in it. It might sound as if we're each tailing around all the time, but in the six years we've been married I've only gotten involved with another woman twice, and as for casual flings, I've gone to bed with someone else less than a dozen times. I'm sure Cathy's score is even less than that."

It wasn't. Cathy had been semi-seriously involved with three men and with a fourth man on a purely sexual level.

"Harold is a sweet man whom I just cannot take seriously," Cathy explains. "He is married and keeps talking about leaving his wife, but he hasn't so far. Well, he's not very handsome, his personality is rather baggy, but in bed he ignites every coal in my body! Apparently he is a real super-stud, because he says other women have told him this also. However, Harold hasn't been around much lately, and when he's not here, I never think about him. As for Karl knowing about what I do, I'm sure he does but he's sweet not to say anything. Sweet and intelligent, because he knows that if he kicked up a storm I'd probably leave him. Karl's attractions as a lover diminish daily while his qualities as a husband and a provider increase inversely. He makes an excellent living, and very generously supplies me with enough money to indulge in all my hobbies and interests. That's one of the reasons I want to keep our marriage going. I know he plays around now and then, but he tries to disguise it and I let him think he has succeeded. You know how I can tell when Karl has been in bed or just necking with another woman? When he comes home, climbs into bed, and immediately starts to make passionate love to me. The last time he did this, I almost laughed at his determination to inflame me with passion, even though he himself was pretty well gassed out emotionally and sexually. I'm sure it has something to do with getting rid of his guilt at having committed adultery—a guilt he still can't forget from his Lutheran childhood. I've been very fortunate in the morals department: I see nothing wrong with extramarital relationships, even when they include sex."

Permissive infidelity is most likely to be found among the wealthy, the creative, the restless, and the self-confident. It flourishes in suburbia as well as in the big city and the small town. Permissive infidelity is a state of mind, not a question of neighborhood. And it must be mutual. If both partners are not in essential agreement, then it no longer is permissive infidelity. It is old-fashioned infidelity.

Chapter Seven

THE IMPACT OF INFIDELITY ON MARRIAGE AND DIVORCE

A standard chunk of dialogue in Hollywood movies and novels until recently involves a husband or wife discovering that the spouse has been unfaithful. "I suppose you'll want a divorce," one of them says, implying that divorce is the inevitable outcome of detected infidelity.

This does indeed still occur, but rarely because of infidelity only. An affair which is discovered dramatically may be the final indignity that shatters a corrupt marriage. However, when two persons have gotten along together reasonably well one episode of infidelity rarely will trigger a divorce. It may produce shock and resentment and sometimes even physical estrangement. But infidelity rarely comes on that suddenly. Its impact on marriage and divorce usually is much slower, a prolonged process closely interwoven with the breakdown of marriage.

Undetected Infidelity

When one partner in a marriage is forced to look outside for unfulfilled needs, one of two changes results: The marriage is strengthened or it is eroded. If the unmet need is satisfactorily supplied extramaritally to the extent that the husband or wife can be free to develop the marital relationship, then both partners have benefited from the infidelity. But when the unmet need is a major one that is satisfied extramaritally, then the husband or wife subconsciously begins to wonder just how important the marriage is. Rarely does infidelity leave a marriage untouched, despite the public protestations of husbands and wives who claim that one or two brief affairs left their marriages unblemished.

Barbara and Gordon were both married when they had a three-day affair at a convention they attended. Its effect on their respective marriages is described by each.

Gordon was twenty-three at the time (he was interviewed eight years later). He had married Janet when he was nineteen and she was twenty, and they both worked until he received his degree in biochemistry. They then had two children rapidly, and a third a few years later.

"Barbara was the first real affair I had since I got married. I had gone to bed with two other women before her, but they were quickies. I felt guilty about them, and as a result I lavished more affection on Janet. By the time I met Barbara at the convention, I was restless in my marriage, but I had no desire to get out of it. Several of the girls at the lab were becoming increasingly attractive to me, and I found myself sitting with other married men in the cafeteria, drooling over the girls, wondering which ones I should try to make at the next convention. I traveled twice yearly as part of my job and spent at least five days out of town. Janet sometimes teased me about being exposed to so many hungry single women and I would laugh it off, but secretly I was hungering for a woman to grab me and seduce me. I'm not a passive man, but I felt so obligated to Janet that I thought it would be necessary for another woman to take me. The moment I met Barbara, of course, I realized that all my daydreams were hooey. She walked up to the exhibit where I was standing and I knew I wanted her. I still cannot understand what she saw in me. I accosted her with the heavy-handed social conversationalities, and when she responded, I threw out my best seductive lines. We had dinner that night, went to a company cocktail party, necked a bit in the cocktail lounge, and separated. The following day we spent entirely together, and that night I made love to her, even though I was terrified at the prospect of disappointing her. She kept assuring me that I was very adequate and that her husband was a clod. The last night of the convention we spent in each other's arms, and I'll never forget the closeness we had.

"I returned home a nervous wreck. It took me four days before I was able to make love to Janet and she sure as hell knew it. Every time I looked at her I saw Barbara, and was terrified that I might call her the wrong name in my sleep. Barbara lived in another state so we had to keep in touch by telephone and letters. We were able to meet again twice that first year, but each time I could sense Janet growing suspicious that I was keeping something from her. I must add that my attitude toward her changed a bit, especially when I compared her with Barbara. Janet has never been what you might call a sexpot; she just sort of puts up with it most of the time, except on those occasions when she's really steamed up, then she can be fun. But Barbara can't get enough. The woman is sexually insatiable. I asked if she was that way with her husband, and she said she had really enjoyed sex with him only twice in their marriage.

"I thought seriously about leaving Janet for Barbara but before I made up my mind, Barbara told me she wanted to cool off our affair for a while. She said she probably would be leaving her husband soon and she didn't want the emotional pressure of having someone else waiting. A few years later she told me that she had been involved with another man off and on just before she met me, but he lived in the same city and seemed like a better prospect. We still see each other a couple of times a year, and we usually manage to go to bed together for a day or two. Barbara is the sexiest woman I know, but I'm glad I'm not married to her, because on non-sexual things like politics, we are in complete disharmony.

"The affair has left its mark on my marriage. Today I'm still not convinced that I should ever be married. I like my privacy and my solitude, which drives Janet nuts. She's been giving me a rather nasty time lately and I'm getting tired of always having to be the one to apologize whenever we have a fight."

Barbara also was affected by her affair with Gordon. According to her, it hastened her out of her marriage and even influenced her decision not to marry a second time.

"I think I probably was more in love with Gordon than he with me, but I was very young then and I didn't know how to show it. I know he was idealizing me because he was discontent with his marriage but didn't know what to do about it. We had a marvelous physical relationship—he was such a tender, warm lover! But after I returned home I could see that my own situation was much too complicated to allow me to enjoy a simple affair with Gordon. I knew that my own marriage was in trouble, and I was involved with another man who wanted me very badly. I felt very wistful at first that Gordon and I could have such a beautiful relationship for those few days before we had to return to reality. Just realizing that such love is possible made me even more determined than before to pry myself loose from a husband whom I no longer loved or respected, and who was really married to his goddamned test tubes.

"After my divorce, I saw Gordon again and I told him that there was another man who was pushing me to marry him. Gordon suggested that I wait a bit since the other man was really breathing down my neck. Gordon's advice turned out to be very valuable, for the moment that I told Stanley (the other man) that I was not about to remarry immediately, he became very ugly. He even threatened to tell my ex-husband about our affair so that I wouldn't get any more alimony. He hounded me so strongly that within a week I threw him out of my life completely.

"I still see Gordon periodically, and we have what I regard as a warm friendship. We sometimes fall right into bed together, while other times we just talk and laugh. I hope I don't imply that Gordon is just a casual friend. He's been a very important part of my life, and my affair with him—I suppose it has never actually stopped even though we cooled down—has shown me that a nice, undemanding love is possible. Even when Gordon does get mad enough to walk out of his marriage, I doubt that I would be willing to marry him. Resume an intense affair with him, yes. Live with him, maybe. But I doubt that we could stay happily married for longer than a few months. And besides, when he gets free, he's going to need months, maybe years to really swing loose and see what he has been missing."

The Flaunted Affair

It is not uncommon for unfaithful individuals to summon the mate's attention by deliberately flaunting an affair under his or her nose. Psychiatrists and marriage counselors are familiar with the husband who is careless with incriminating evidence, hoping his wife will become suspicious and discover the affair. There are wives who are equally blatant in advertising their extramarital activities.

Some men interviewed for this study claimed that such flaunting was their way of forcing the hand of a wife who refused to acknowledge that a marriage was in trouble. There are other men who want the wife to be the one to dissolve the marriage, thus relieving them of guilt and enabling them to plead innocence to children, relatives, and friends.

It's necessary to distinguish between hopeless marriages and just dull marriages in considering the brazen affair. The husband or wife in a bad marriage probably flaunts infidelity to provoke the spouse and speed up dissolution of the marriage. Where the marriage is merely boring, an affair may be displayed to shake an indifferent partner out of lethargy, or force both partners to pay more attention to the marriage and see if it might be improved.

The effect intended is not always the effect achieved. The wife whose husband is parading an affair under her nose to make her more attentive to him may find that she has been disgusted with the marriage for some time, and this brazenness provides the opportunity to throw him out of the house and file for a divorce. Or a wife who is trying to provoke her husband into walking out on her may find herself trapped in the marriage when her husband uses the detected affair as emotional blackmail, threatening to reveal all to children, parents, relatives, and friends.

Accidental Detection

When one partner discovers for the first time that a spouse is having an affair—particularly when it is sexual—the reaction often is profound shock followed by hurt and sometimes even guilt. Just as the deliberate flaunting of an affair can produce a nasty backlash, so an accidentally discovered affair can leave permanent scars on a marriage or divorce.

The one unpredictable element in an otherwise perfect infidelity is the danger of accidental detection. An automobile accident, a fire in the motel, a heart attack, a fall in a strange shower, being seen by a friend—any one of these can happen and voila! discreet infidelity has become flagrant adultery.

Two other forms of accidental detection—pregnancy without marital intercourse and venereal disease—are less common but equally damning. Whatever the cause, accidental detection invariably touches off fireworks in a marriage, sometimes even devastating explosions. The individuals interviewed for this book agree that, in their experiences, accidentally discovered infidelity is much more damaging when the spouse already suspects infidelity and may be thinking about a divorce. In only one case did such infidelity disrupt an otherwise happy marriage.

June had depended emotionally and financially on her husband, Art, throughout the eight years of their marriage. Both had married in their late twenties with relatively little experience with the other sex. Art was a graphic arts designer who was not given to loud conversation. He was sociable to the extent of attending parties and drinking heartily, but he rarely said much. June was his greatest admirer, even after they were married, and at every lull in the conversation she would step in to sing his praises. Art discouraged this, and their mutual friends concluded that June kept it up because of strong feelings of inferiority.

Art traveled about six times a year, and every time he visited the headquarters city of his firm, he managed to visit the local whorehouse. Art liked to try everything once, and he found that patronizing the brothel was easier than explaining his curiosity to June, whom he called "a real meat-and-potatoes girl when it comes to sex, while I'm a gourmet."

After a few visits, the madam recognized Art and treated him as a favored client. He tried something different every trip, and always tipped the madam when he left. "It's probably one of the few clean whorehouses left in the United States and I'm doing my part to see that this noble institution does not disappear from the American scene. Also, it's cheaper than patronizing prostitutes or call girls, and with a whorehouse whore you know what you're getting and the management stands behind its services."

Art insisted that he visited the whorehouse to gratify his curiosity as well as to avoid being unfaithful to June, whom he loved and did not want to hurt.

It was Art's misfortune to be in the whorehouse the one night that it was raided. The madam had forgotten to pay off the police, and since the newly elected district attorney had campaigned on a policy of cleaning up the city, the brothel was raided and all the girls, the madam, and the customers were hauled off in a patrol wagon. At the station, the customers were released after identifying themselves, and Art gratefully returned to his hotel, reassured by the desk sergeant that his name would not be given out.

That wasn't quite true, for the local paper printed the story on Page One the following afternoon, and within a few days the article made its way via friend and foe to June, who showed it without comment to Art one night after supper.

Realizing that he was indeed caught with his pants down, Art admitted everything, telling June exactly why he went to the brothel. He expected her to be upset and maybe even angry, but when he was through she just smiled, walked to the closet, and pulled out three suitcases which she had filled with his clothes and personal effects.

"Get out immediately, you pig!" June snarled. "And don't you dare try to touch me while you're leaving because I don't want to be contaminated! When I think of how you have touched me after being pawed by those slimy whores, I could kill you! Just take your belongings, get out of here, and don't ever let me see you or hear your voice again. If you have anything to say, call my lawyer."

Art left and June was as good as her word. She did everything possible to destroy all traces of him in her life, including cutting off joint friendships. She deliberately looked for and found the meanest lawyer in the county and, dangling a handsome retainer under his nose, told him to bring back Art's hide. To his credit as a divorce lawyer (and his disgrace as a human being) the lawyer did his best to crucify Art by having him followed, bugging his apartment, and even hiring a prostitute to try to pick him up and take him to a hotel room which the lawyer, a witness, and a photographer would raid.

But one of Art's friends, also a lawyer, learned by accident that June wanted not only to divorce him but to hurt him as badly as possible, and he tipped off Art. With the connivance of several imaginative friends, Art sandbagged the lawyer with his own tricks. It turned out that the lawyer was so used to looking for dirt in other people's lives that he was careless about exposing his own. It was a simple matter to photograph him with various female companions, none of whom was his wife. Also, Art and his friends found a young prostitute who, for $25, was willing to try to pick up the lawyer in a bar he was known to frequent a few evenings a month. The plan worked beautifully, the lawyer swallowed the bait and went to the hooker's apartment. Art's friends got several incriminating telephoto shots and, instead of breaking in, had the prostitute turn on a tape recorder once they were in the bedroom.

The next day, Art walked into the lawyer's office while his wife was consulting him. June was furious and ordered Art out. The lawyer, deferring to the source of his fee, became abusive and told him to get out or he would call the police. With June staring in horror, Art stretched out photographic prints of her lawyer in a variety of compromising poses, then he switched on his tape recorder. The lawyer withdrew from the case that morning.

This sounds wildly imaginative but it is true. With the exceptions of a few details to disguise it a bit, it is a factual case history. Its inclusion in this chapter may help explain why Art's infidelity at the whorehouse touched off such vindictive fury in a wife who until their separation had seemed so devoted to him. Although her reaction may have been in part a revulsion against the idea of sharing a man with a woman she regarded as unclean, most of their mutual friends concluded that June became insanely furious with Art for having exposed her to ridicule among her family and friends. She was crushed that people she admired and respected now knew that she had married a man who would slink into a whorehouse, orgy for hours, then sneak back to his wife's bed.

"IF YOU CAN DO IT, SO CAN I!"

When infidelity surfaces in a marriage already riddled with bitterness and antagonism, the previously monogamous mate sometimes will respond by seeking an opportunity to be unfaithful. This often is frustration and a desire for vengeance, but sometimes it serves as an excuse to practise what the offended spouse had been thinking about but repressing. An attractive wife whose husband is involved with other women probably has been exposed to other men and opportunities to experiment in infidelity. When it becomes obvious to her that her husband sees nothing wrong with extramarital affairs, she looks to the most obvious sources: her neighbors, interested men in any organization or club she might belong to, or even her husband's friends. One thirty-seven-year-old man who has lived as a bachelor for almost ten years since his divorce, admits that he specializes in consoling unhappy wives.

"I've lived in many large cities and I've never found any shortage of married women to lead to bed. Actually they're more abundant than single women or divorcées, and they're not necessarily looking for another husband. Oh sure, they may be hunting, but they've still got a husband to dispose of, children to worry about, and so forth. And it's increasingly easier to find them. All I have to do is join a number of groups like political clubs, folk-dancing societies, adult-education classes (particularly those in film-making, photography, and art—these seem to really draw the dissatisfied housewives), and the pickings are marvelous."

In one city he concentrated on folk dancing; in another he joined the Young Democrats and several adult-education classes, and in still another he found that the little theater groups and art classes were the most fertile. On a recent visit, he opened his wallet and disclosed more than one hundred membership cards for everything ranging from the Ethical Culture Society to the Sierra Club.

"My tactics are quite simple. I join an organization and show up at a few meetings. Then I attend every possible social function where there will be more than twenty people present. If it's a political club that I'm in, I wait until an election is approaching, and the parties usually are overflowing. In little theater groups, I make the opening night parties, the business meetings, or the cast parties for the shows. Parties are the important part of my scheme, and I rarely join a club or group that does not throw at least impromptu parties.

"When I attend a party, it is not hard to pick out the unhappily married women. They usually are with one friend, they smile at even the most asinine statement, and they still have their wedding rings on. But even though they smile, they don't hang on every word in the simpering manner of the unmarried or divorced women. Sometimes, they can be spotted by the fact that they're preoccupied about something—usually their marriages.

"Once I establish rapport with a married woman, I let her know as rapidly as possible that I am not married. This clearly establishes that I am not another of those rotten bastard husbands out for a fast piece of ass. My singleness is a real blessing and I exploit it to the hilt, as it were. If I like a woman and the sparks are starting to fly, I try to get her away from the party as rapidly as possible. I don't care where we go but I insist on getting her out of there. It breaks the ties with girl friends, mutual acquaintances who might say something to the husband, and the attitude that she must remain properly uninterested in men she meets through the group.

"If she is unwilling to leave, I try to get her to commit herself to a meeting in the next few days. If she is coy and refuses, I then ask her for her telephone number and cross her off my mental list. I don't want or need a woman who is uncertain about what she wants to do, for such wives may decide at the last minute that they really cannot betray their husbands, or they will cover my shoulder with tears and ask me to be patient with them while they work out their lives.

"When I do get a woman away from the party, I make it clear to her that I want to make love to her. This may seem crude, but it immediately defines my interest and eliminates the silly little games. Surprisingly, the majority of women who throw off sparks to me appreciate this candor and ultimately end up in my bed. Married women seem so much less hung up than their single sisters about trying out a relationship in bed before it progresses further. If sexual compatibility is not there, why sweat through weeks or months of getting to know someone, only to be disappointed at the moment of truth? This incidentally is their philosophy, one which they have taught me. If there is a potential closeness, it will show up in bed, and so far I have been wrong about this only three or four times in the last ten years.

"Sexually, I am very easily satisfied, but if I can satisfy a strange woman to whom I am attracted, I am triply delighted. So many of the married women I have taken to bed have said afterwards that if only their husbands would work half as hard as I did, they would never have started looking elsewhere. It is a sad commentary on my own sex that husbandhood seems to confer dullness and sexual incompetence. I say this because it is not uncommon for a married woman to suggest marriage with me after the third or fourth date. I don't want to steal any man's wife, nor do I want to marry again, but damnit, there should be a book written for husbands about how sexually hungry their wives are. I'm not a particularly spectacular lover, but I am willing to keep working on a woman until she's thoroughly aroused. Also, I have found that even the most conservative housewife enjoys variety in sex. She loves to be eaten—something her husband rarely does or else only with obvious disgust. She enjoys being tickled and played with to the point of screaming. And more than anything, she wants a man who can stay in her for more than thirty seconds without blasting off. I can't offer any advice on this subject except practise. I now can hold back my orgasm for as long as I want—something I never could do with my former wife. I was thirty years old before I could do this, but it was worth waiting for. I've ended up in bed with many women who complain that their husbands' only flaw has been premature ejaculation. Even if a man comes quickly, he can spend lots of time getting his wife warmed up and excited before he actually enters her."

What about husbands who discover that their wives are being unfaithful, at least to the extent of forming close personal relationships with other men? Their reactions tend to be similar but not nearly so dramatic as the frustrated wives. The cuckolded husband often is the ineffective husband. Like the man quoted above, there are single women who thrive on married men who are dissatisfied at home. Marybeth is one such woman. She is thirty-three, unmarried, and experienced with single as well as married men. Not nearly as specific as the bachelor who preys on married women, Marybeth still thinks of marriage and hopes that she might meet a man who will whisk her off to a dream house in the suburbs. But as the years advance, Marybeth concedes that such a possibility is fading.

"I don't really look for married men, but they seem to be attracted to me. I meet them constantly at parties and in my work. When one that I am attracted to is coming on very strong, why should I turn him off because he is unhappily married? In the last few years I've been involved with maybe six married men whose wives were playing around and who decided to try their hands at it.

"The more involved with a man I become, the more my feminine survival instincts take over. When I find myself in love with a man, I want him, and I'll do everything possible to pry him away from his wife. Sure I make demands on his time, and if he can't meet these demands, then I am angry. Why should I sit in my apartment all weekend, cooling my heels, while he is playing the domestic bliss game? Goddamn it, I want him to spend every free moment with me and to hell with that bitch in her ranch house with her snotty-nose kids, the mortgage, and her bridge tournament. And when she has been playing around with other men, I cannot understand why her husband should deny me what I ask. I don't want mink coats, cars, or any of the kept-woman crap—just him. If she plays, why shouldn't he? But so many husbands are supercharged with guilt and domestic docility that they creep home to Mamma after a pleasant evening in my bed.

"It's really pathetic to see that these men are only looking for a woman to hold them and love them, a woman who is sexually adventuresome, and a woman who can bring out their fullest sexuality. American wives are horrible flops, for I've been able to satisfy a number of husbands who claim that their wives would never dream of doing what to me is perfectly natural. If I love a man, I want to feel him, taste him, and stimulate him to the highest possible degree, because a stimulated man is a good lover, and that is what I am after.

"It's funny, but the things married men ask me to do are so insignificant that I cannot understand why their wives refuse them. Some insist that I leave my stockings on while we make love. Others prefer oral eroticism as a prelude, which I find enormously pleasing. I've met men who were violently turned on by a woman taking off her clothes and climbing on top of them. One man even insisted that he and I ceremoniously remove one another's clothing, but he turned out to be one of the best lovers I have ever had, so perhaps there is something in his method. Another man, whose wife always used a diaphragm, insisted on using condoms, and seemed to get pleasure from it. But the most stimulating experience I ever had was with Rudy, a married man whose wife had told him that he was an inadequate lover and that she intended to look for a better one. Rudy and I got pleasantly drunk one night and returned to my apartment. He worked on me for maybe two hours to the point where I wanted him. But instead of making love to me, Rudy tied my arms and legs to the bed posts and covered my breasts and pubic region with raspberry preserves. I really thought he might be a bit nuts when he started to lick. Within moments, I was thrashing and throbbing, screaming at him to stop. When he finally gave me what I wanted, I was the sexiest creature in the world and he knew it. He stayed with me that night because I demanded it. We made love at least twelve times that weekend and when it came time for him to leave, I was an admitted husband-stealer. I wanted him as a lover and I couldn't imagine him going back to that drab, bitchy wife in her split-level home. His children could rot in hell as far as I was concerned. I took off from work Monday and just lolled around the apartment, hoping he would call. Finally, I called him and told him I was panting for his body. He hemmed a good deal, then said that he really had to mend fences at home. I screamed at him that his wife was out screwing other men and how could he deny me after such an incredible weekend. I kept hoping that he would show up, but by late Monday night I knew that I was dealing with a married man.

"He still is hanging in with his marriage, even though his wife now is talking about divorce. He visits me maybe once a month, and we spend an enjoyable night, but he always romps back to suburbia and the family. I've recovered somewhat from my passion and I know now that he is at best an occasional lover. But damn his eyes, he is miserably married and I'd like to shake him out of it."

APPEALING TO A THIRD PARTY

When a marriage is teetering on the verge of dissolution, an episode of infidelity can send one or both partners to a disinterested referee—usually a psychiatrist, a marriage counselor, or a friendly lawyer.

The problem with such referees is that they are expected to take sides. The psychiatrist is concerned with his patient and not the spouse. The lawyer tries to be objective but must keep an eye open for the legal advantages of his client, who also may be a friend. The marriage counselor wants to hear both sides of a dispute even though both partners may be so argued out that they cannot stand another rehashing. Also, with a marriage counselor listening, the husband or wife may try to impress him by being clever, by lying, by provoking the partner to an intemperate outburst, and by otherwise distorting the situation.

It is reasonable to say that marriage counselors are useful for those couples who sincerely want to keep their marriages together, whereas psychiatrists can be helpful when one partner is worried about his or her own behavior. The lawyer is consulted when divorce is being contemplated—usually when a marriage is dead and needs to be formally buried.

The advantage of appealing to a third person is the classical need to be able to talk about intensely personal problems, preferably without running the risk of moral censure. This is one of the reasons why clergymen usually hear only the "innocent" side of a diseased marriage.

The difficulty with such consultation is that it costs

money and while advice may be handed out, it really is neither wanted nor followed. The husband and wife who want to save their marriage may well go to a marriage counselor, but they know where the problems lie, and having someone else point them out may provide a face-saving solution. However, it generally is true that once a marriage is sour, no amount of third-party refereeing will salvage it. Marriage counselors have become skilled at spotting the argumentative couple and separating them for private sessions, bringing them together only when there seems some likelihood of agreement.

While the marriage counselor works best with both partners in a marriage, the psychiatrist prefers to work with only one. There are some psychiatrists who will see husband and wife separately, but they are the exception. Psychiatric help is directed at the individual so that he can discover why he acts the way he does, what he wants from the marriage, and what he is giving to it. Many husbands and wives claim that psychotherapy has saved their marriages, while others report that it helped to point out the futility of the marriage and hastened a divorce. The chief disadvantage of psychiatric counseling for many is its cost: A single one-hour session in a psychiatrist's office costs anywhere from $20 to $100, and psychotherapy usually requires months of weekly sessions.

Psychiatrists and Infidelity

Because of their involvement as listeners in infidelity, psychiatrists and clinical psychologists sometimes are thrown into the interesting position of having to react professionally to a person they find personally or physically stimulating. A psychiatrist is not a machine, and he may have profound marital problems of his own. Several former wives or mistresses of psychiatrists were interviewed for this project, and their comments illustrated the sad dilemma of professional individuals who also are human.

It is not unusual to meet a woman who has gone to bed with her psychotherapist, nor is it uncommon to find psychiatrists and psychologists who have rotten marriages. After all, the therapist is in an ideal situation when he has a patient who is baring her soul in the complete privacy of his office. Some women report starting affairs in the office, while others say they have been pursued after office hours by the therapist. Three women reported successful seductions of or by their psychiatrists during the great power blackout of November, 1965, in the northeast section of the country.

Julie, a thrice-married artist, had been in therapy for eight months when the blackout hit. Her psychiatrist's office was on the 29th floor of a New York skyscraper, and the power failure left them stranded for more than six hours.

"Our session had just ended and I was putting on my coat when the lights flickered, then went out. I didn't think much about it, and walked out to the elevator. After a few minutes of standing there, my psychiatrist came out of his office and said that there seemed to be no electricity. He invited me to return and wait until power was restored. We sat in his office—not in our usual therapy places—and chatted for an hour or so. Somebody from an office down the hall poked his head in and told us about the blackout after hearing it on a transistor radio. We just laughed and continued chatting. He opened up his liquor cabinet and we started drinking. After a while, we were sitting together on the couch, pretending we were strangers and offering instant analyses of each other's characters from superficial comments. The game was fun, and as we continued, we seemed to draw closer together. I wasn't thinking very clearly, for my session with him had really been quite draining. The next thing I knew, we were kissing passionately, then he was removing my sweater. I was stunned that he would condescend to make love to me, even though I was very excited over him. I think the shock of being made love to by a man I regarded as aloof and godlike made me seem like a limp rag to him. Actually, I was tremendously excited. We made love, but it was a bit of a disappointment. I'm sure I expected too much, and it was a shock to see him as a man."

Julie never went back to her psychiatrist, for she got embroiled in the tail end of a nasty divorce suit and she didn't think she could face the psychiatrist again. Other women, however, have been able to carry on brisk affairs with their therapists, some of them converting them into free psychiatric consultations.

"Why the hell should I pay him to blow the cobwebs out of my mind unles he pays me for blowing him every week?" one wife asked.

The psychiatrist away from his office is a different creature. At home, he theoretically is just another husband, but the wives of psychiatrists claim that this is not necessarily true.

"These men analyze their patients and themselves silly," one ex-wife of a psychiatrist says. "They're incapable of doing something or thinking something without analyzing it to pieces. When I would grab my husband passionately, so help me God, he would ask me with a straight face why I was doing it. On one occasion shortly before we separated, I waited until he was just about to come and I suddenly froze, looked at him, and asked him why he was carrying on so. Another time, I inquired if he thought he was screwing his mother. This really made him mad, but it was the sort of comment that he constantly kept throwing at me. My experience makes me warn girls who are thinking of marrying psychiatrists that they will have to be either mindless doormats or objects of constant analysis. I didn't mind what Jack said to his patients, but when he started giving me the same treatment in bed, I revolted and ultimately left him."

The clinical psychologist seems to be less problem as a mate than the psychiatrist, perhaps because the psychiatrist must spend eight years getting his M.D., followed by a psychiatric residency of three to five years, whereas the clinical psychologist needs only a Ph.D., although there are "lay analysts" who possess varying academic qualifications. The real difference between a psychiatrist and a clinical psychologist is that medical students tend to live monkish existences, insulated from their fellow-men, whereas student psychologists need not live in such a rarefied atmosphere. This is a broad generalization, but it is supported by the testimony of wives and husbands of both psychiatrists and psychologists.

Lawyers and Infidelity

The role played by the divorce lawyer in shattering marriages will be discussed fully in the next chapter, but here we are concerned with the lawyer whose professional zeal is outweighed by his passions and he goes to bed with a client. It is not uncommon for an attorney to be moved to action by an attractive but maritally unhappy client. She may not yet be ready for a divorce but only wants information. She is pretty and pathetic; he is wise and comforting. The situation is ideal, especially since professional ethics (if divorce lawyers can be said to have any, compared with other professions) do not frown on the attorney's continuing discussion of the case over a cocktail, then over dinner. When the attorney himself is bored with his marriage, he has excellent opportunity to avail himself of clients in need of comfort as well as legal advice. And what is doubly charming about the easy ethics of the bar is that a lawyer who takes his client to bed can, with a straight face, bill her for his time.

"That son of a bitch sent me a bill for $50 after we had spent most of the evening in bed. He said it was for legal advice, and I reminded him that most of his advice was dispensed with his pants off. If I weren't afraid that my husband would try to get custody of the children, I'd report that lawyer to the bar. He finally agreed not to press for payment of the bill, but rather to transfer it to my husband when I did actually file for divorce, explaining that the husband usually has to pay for the wife's attorney. I cannot stand my husband, but I don't think he should get financially screwed for my getting it physically. I wonder how many divorce lawyers are doing this? I have asked some of my girl friends who have been through divorces, and this apparently is very common. One of them had a lawyer who offered to handle her case without fee if she would spend several nights in bed with him. She was naïve as hell and she agreed. What she didn't know is that the bastard just sent the bill to her husband. And he collected, too!"

Clients whose relations with their attorneys have been sexual as well as legal may have made the best of a nasty situation, but the majority of divorced men and women harbor evil thoughts for the attorneys involved. Some ex-husbands cannot speak of divorce lawyers without choking up, and there are many divorcées who feel that they were gouged and poorly represented through the whole business. Some women deliberately flirt with their attorneys, hoping to stir enough interest in them so that their fees will be lowered. And surprisingly, some husbands report that they have attempted to whet the appetites of their wives' lawyers by describing them in exciting terms.

"I knew my wife's attorney better than she did," reports an ex-husband who got out of his marriage with a minimum of trauma and financial disaster. "I also knew that he wasn't too happy with his wife, whom everyone regarded as a cold fish. So when I went to see him the first time, I played the sexually dominated husband. Swearing him to secrecy, I let him in on the embarrassing fact that Marilyn was just too oversexed for me. I mean, I liked it once or twice a week, but she was crawling all over me every night. I also implied that she looked up to older men—he was at least ten years older than I was. All this was a crock of crap, of course. Marilyn is sensuous as hell, but so am I, and we never had much trouble about supply and demand in bed. We just had violently clashing personalities.

"I didn't tell Marilyn what I was doing but I did build up her lawyer to her. It worked beautifully! He fell for the buildup and started flirting with her. She responded and they both were out for dinner and into bed before a week was out. During the negotiations, I told my lawyer that I was damned if I would pay the legal fee for a man who was adulterously sleeping with my wife and that this was one concession I would not make. Well, her lawyer was in no position to insist that I pay his fee, so Marilyn had to pay it. And he didn't dare send her more than a token bill, because he had spent more time in bed with her than in the office. I have seen friends go through utter hell at the hands of those chartered crooks known as divorce lawyers, and my advice is to beat them by making them part of your own marital mess. They're shrewd but basically stupid, and they find it hard to resist an invitation into bed."

While divorce lawyers may object to this man's attitude toward their craft, the experiences of other husbands and wives point to an easily exploited vulnerability on the part of these attorneys. Of course, there are lawyers who only occasionally see a divorce through the courts, and these comments are not necessarily directed toward them so much as the men who specialize in divorce.

Appealing to Friends and Relatives

When friends and relatives start hearing all the horrors of a bad marriage, it has advanced one step closer toward dissolution. The effect of these confidences may be just the opposite of what is intended. Instead of rallying to the side of the injured or offended partner, relatives and friends often draw back. Those who have ever been exposed to an exploding marriage have little desire to get hit by the shrapnel. The easiest way to avoid involvement in a domestic crisis is to refuse to comment or take sides. Friends generally assume the attitude that the couple should work out their problems themselves, without calling on them for help. Relatives sometimes feel obligated to take sides, but if they do they usually gain one enemy for every friend.

This refusal to get involved is painful to the unhappily married person, for he or she needs to be able to talk to someone who is sympathetic yet who will not offer unacceptable advice. The disinterested third party is one solution, but for reasons of economy or personal need, certain married men and women turn to relatives and friends. One curiously common reaction is that when neighbors, business colleagues, and friends learn that a marriage is in danger, they often move in on the husband or wife in order to take advantage of the crisis. Some observers regard this simply as an extension of the killer instinct which causes creatures of a species to close in on a wounded member of the pack. Several divorced women report that male friends and neighbors closed in on them as soon as they discovered that the marriage was going down the drain, or that they or their husbands had been involved in infidelity.

"It seemed that because Herb had been having an affair with his secretary I should be anxious to get into bed with every man I knew," complained a forty-year-old divorcée. Men who suddenly reveal that their marriages have gone sour, or who are known to be involved with other women often find themselves the objects of attention from single or divorced women around them. Bill, a production manager in a southern publishing firm, found that once his intended divorce became known around the office, several women who had treated him with distance or respect now approached him, flirted with him, and tried to coax him to date them.

"I went out with a few, and one of them was really trying hard to get me stirred up. Just as we were getting out of bed she started asking what was in this affair for her, and how she stood with me. I discovered that she was talking about marriage. I backed out of that one before I could get emotionally involved, and I discovered that the other girls all were thinking along the same lines, but they weren't about to let themselves get involved unless I was willing to fall in love with them. Then they'd be interested in a hot and heady affair. It's funny, but I keep hearing complaints from men who can't get something going with women. I want to tell them to open up and announce their availability, then jump into the first opportunity for emotional involvement. It may get sticky as hell, but it'll be fun!"

Infidelity and Children

A family in which infidelity has developed fully probably is an unhappy family. Husband and wife are at each other's throats, and children sense that something is wrong. Even when the parents are careful not to argue in front of the children, the atmosphere of distrust and hostility is strong enough to be picked up even by a tiny youngster. And when the parents don't bother to hide their arguments from the children, they are likely to sling around some strong accusations. Parents of both sexes who have been involved in infidelity-provoked battles agree unanimously that individually, each one could have exercised enough self-control to hold off until the children were out of earshot, but the spouse unfortunately lacked such discipline and didn't give a damn whether the children could hear or not.

Such exposure to parental nastiness may provoke a child into choosing sides, especially when he knows that the parents probably will be breaking up.

Children also can be the ultimate weapon. Used by a clever spouse, they can innocently instill heavy doses of guilt in the other parent. A woman may be pushing hard to get rid of her husband, but she can't let him go without hurting him just a bit more. So she coaches the children to plead with him not to desert them. His wife is shoving him out the door, he wants to get far away from her, and here his children are begging him to stay. He usually leaves, but with a heavy load of guilt and remorse.

There are spouses who will continue to use the children after a divorce has been granted. Frank, a forty-year-old father of four, was summarily kicked out of his home by his wife, Judith, after nearly fifteen years of marriage. The reasons for the divorce are not pertinent and both agree they are happier apart. But Frank, anxious to louse up Judith's life as he believes she has loused up his, used their children to discourage her from remarrying. Frank took advantage of his visitation time with the children to arouse their fears about a new man moving into the house. He taught them how to discourage Judith's suitors (she was stunningly attractive and had more than one eligible male after her), and how to plead with her not to marry again.

Men Who Hang on to Bad Marriages

A recurring question from both men and women is why many men have such difficulty breaking away from a bad marriage. Men who themselves have hung on for years wonder whether they are masochists or just guilt-ridden. And the women who have made the decisive step in breaking up a marriage cannot understand their husbands' refusal to take that step or their obvious relief to be out of the marriage. No matter how badly some men want a divorce, they seem incapable of forcing the break.

This question was immediately recognized by a large percentage of the men and women interviewed for this study, and they attempted to answer it.

There is no doubt that guilt plays a prominent role in a husband's reluctance to leave his wife. Guilt toward her and guilt toward the children were cited by men who had encountered this difficulty. Economics also are an important consideration, and often are mentioned very early in a conversation about why the man has not left or else taken so long to leave.

Deep probing turned up the fact that many men do not want to be the ones to make the break. They want the wife to decide that the marriage is dead and make the first step toward separation and divorce. If the man can shift the responsibility for the actual break to the wife, he often then will be surprisingly happy to be free both of the marriage *as well as the token responsibility for the breakup.*

In considering a divorce men seem to dread loneliness much more than women do. Even men who later have been relieved to be alone and free to enjoy themselves fully with a variety of women admit that the prospects of loneliness frightened them when they first thought about divorce.

Some men who desperately want to be free from the marriage but cannot bring themselves to make the break try to subtly nudge their wives in that direction. This may involve deliberately provoking vicious quarrels or reviving long-dormant issues. A less subtle way is to leave incriminating letters, notes, or telephone numbers where a wife is certain to find them.

The pathetic aspect about these men—and they are numerous—is that no amount of prodding by friends, neighbors, or business associates will get them to take that single step. Only when the wife says (and means it) that the marriage is over, will these husbands breathe easy again.

Such men often are very attractive to other women who recognize their marital dissatisfaction and think they can easily pry them loose from their wives. They are eager to swing and they talk freely about divorce and remarriage, for that is what they really want. However, getting them to actually leave a marriage has taxed the patience of countless Other Women. The typical extramarital girl friend of such husbands usually thinks it will be a matter of months before he gets out of the marriage and enters another. To bring this about, the Other Woman has to be a superb tactician, willing to accept delays and infuriating setbacks. She has to think about years instead of months if she is realistic.

And most important, she must abandon her traditional

posture of the disinterested observer waiting demurely for her man to come to her. Humiliating though it may seem to her, she must take an active role in applying the *coup de grâce* to a dying marriage. She must connive and scheme with her lover to provide him with all the ammunition he needs to make the break or to force his wife to leave him, frequently the latter. If she loves the man sufficiently and is willing to sacrifice some of her pride, she can bring this about. Relying solely on him invites disappointment and heartbreak.

The man involved in such an affair is acutely aware of the unstated pressure from his girl friend to get out of the marriage. Yet he cannot, except as a supreme sacrifice, and he does not want to lay his psyche out for mutilation. He wants support even though he dare not ask for it. He wants suggestions and ways to force a break. If the Other Woman is willing to give these cheerfully and without hostility, she stands a good chance of success. Her willingness to participate in helping the man overcome this one weakness may also influence the degree of happiness the two will enjoy once he is free from his marriage.

Chapter Eight

THE UBIQUITOUS THIRD PARTY— THE LAWYER

No discussion of divorce lawyers should begin without first noting that lawyers have a vested interest in breaking up marriages. Should a couple, despite the best advice of an attorney, choose to reconcile, all the lawyer gets is a token fee and the taste of ashes in his mouth.

Also, it should be noted that lawyers are among those who have the most cause to oppose the idea of infidelity substituting for divorce. Divorce, that is, in the painful American tradition, replete with legal ritual, unintelligible language, child support, alimony, separation agreements, visitation rights, property settlement, division of personal possessions, income-support escalation clauses, and most important, handsome fees for two deserving attorneys.

If any reader thinks that the lawyer has been unjustly treated in this book, let him conduct a dozen quick interviews of the beneficiaries of legal services connected with divorce. There is a widespread hatred and contempt for divorce lawyers (who prefer that they be described as "specialists in matrimonial or family law") that really should command the public relations energies of the American Bar Association to counter, for things have gotten so far out of hand that there are proposals afoot in many states to shoehorn lawyers right out of the divorce business. The argument of many divorce reform groups is that a lawyer is not needed to get married so why bring him in to dissolve a marriage? Anti-lawyer groups are particularly incensed at the adversary system incorporated in most prevailing divorce laws that requires one party to emerge innocent while the other is guilty, even though the divorce is mutually agreeable.

Since laws are written by lawyers, it is no surprise that an attorney is required even when a divorce is uncontested. And the attorney, who may do less than a day's work on the case, naturally expects to collect his fee.

"Look, divorce lawyers are the Mafia of the legal profession," insists a tax attorney who himself has been through two divorces. "Divorce law attracts the same sort of men who become gangsters, cops, prison guards, process servers, or automobile repossessors. They're swine, and like Henry Adams said about politicians, you don't reason with them. You just hit them on the nose with a stick. In my own practise, I would consider handling an uncontested divorce for a friend, provided I was dealing with another lawyer who did not make his living from busting up marriages. What galls me and galls so many of my clients who have had to patronize the divorce boys is the way they seem to thrive on misery.

"They're positively obscene as they figure out ways to strip couples of every remaining cent, and surround the dissolution of a marriage with every possible indignity. When first in love, two persons walk hand in hand through a smiling world. When they have discovered that they really cannot live together, they're thrown to the grinning, bow-tied jackals with their lists of private detectives and all the other business surrounding divorce."

Many of those interviewed for this book claimed that

when confronted with a borderline marriage, the divorce lawyer will subtly push it toward divorce. There is no problem when both parties want to get out of the marriage as fast as possible. Then, all that is necessary is for the attorneys to get together, divide up the joint property, work out settlements, and then submit their bills. When they are wealthy or famous, such clients may find themselves faced with enormous legal fees. This is the old "ability-to-pay" concept that various professions have been pushing for years. In other words, the more you have, the more you should pay for the services of a lawyer, a physician, an accountant, or anyone else who can get away with this line. The inequity in this concept is that while the fees have no top limit, they definitely have a bottom and will not dip below the bare minimum—in divorce, usually $250. That figure is for an uncontested divorce in which the attorney puts in a minimum of work. When the client is wealthy, attorneys often find many complicated little chores that must be done and that jack up the fee accordingly. And no two attorneys charge the same fee. For example, an estranged wife in Connecticut was charged $1,500 by her attorney whereas her husband in New York City had to pay only $250. This was for an uncontested divorce.

Couples who are separating or divorcing are at the mercy of the attorneys, for there is no review board before which to complain of exorbitantly high fees. As the twice-divorced attorney phrased it, "when it comes to collecting fees, the divorce boys have you right by the balls, for if you don't come up with their money, they don't file the final papers, and you have no divorce and everything is unresolved."

The growing horror of formerly married persons with the unbelievable mumbo-jumbo that American divorce has become has prompted divorce reform groups to go a step farther and call for the exclusion of lawyers from divorce cases except where there is a clear case of legal dispute.

Fighting Dirty

Perhaps the quality that most disturbs laymen about the divorce lawyers is their penchant for fighting dirty, for aiming well below the belt, and for not hesitating to kick a downed opponent in the face. The lawyers reply in hurt innocence that this is all part of the game, part of the legal ritual in which they are the high priests. What they don't seem to understand or want to understand is that the unhappily married couple wants to dissolve the marriage with as little ceremony and fuss as possible.

A strong complaint against lawyers from divorced men and women is that they seem so insensitive to the fact that they are dealing with human beings with delicate emotions. They will encourage a wife to have her husband served with divorce papers or a court injunction while he is playing peacefully with the children in the living room, because that is the one time when the husband's guard is completely down.

Or the wife whose estranged husband has fallen behind in child support may be encouraged by her lawyer to invite the husband back for a warm, friendly talk, and possibly even a reconciliation. At the lawyer's instigation, she already has sworn out a warrant for his arrest and the police march into her apartment, seize him, and drag him off to jail. And what is the response of the divorce attorney?

"Too bad. If he doesn't keep up with his child support he deserves to go to jail. It'll teach him a lesson!"

Disillusioned veterans of divorce have to be reminded that this is not just the divorce lawyer speaking, but every lawyer—the man who invented laws and jails to enforce them. Part of the system that lawyers have encouraged to enforce the laws they make involves raping the human being of every last stitch of human dignity, the better to reduce him to a fearful, pleading supplicant for mercy. That way he is grateful for any bone flung to him by the august majesty of the law, as represented by a judge or lawyer.

Those who have been through nasty divorces are appalled at the power an attorney has at his fingertips, especially where the opposing party is unwilling to hire or unable to afford a lawyer. Divorce court judges are notoriously partial to whatever an attorney says, and they have no compunction about clapping a man in jail for falling behind in alimony or child support, even though he is unable to earn any money while in jail. This incredible vestige of debtors' prison can be found in parts of the United States.

"If I had known what vicious bastards would be getting their fangs into my neck when I filed for divorce, I would simply have reconciled with my wife," a thirty-eight-year-old accountant recalled.

"Jean and I agreed that it would be best to separate and see whether we might be happier divorced. It was all very amicable, except that she asked for a stiff hunk of my salary as support for the two kids and herself. I did my damnedest to pay it in full and on time, but sometimes I was a few days late, and occasionally I had to send a bit less because I was so strapped for money. When it became apparent that we both wanted a divorce, I knew that I'd need more money so I accepted a transfer to our New York office which would give me a nice raise in salary so that I could afford to send Jean enough money.

"But in the meantime, she had gone to a lawyer and told him how much I was giving her. He immediately sent me forms and letters which would bind me to send exactly that amount and no less, and if I didn't, authorize him to attach my wages and all sorts of other insane things. When he heard that I was going to be making more money after my transfer, he wrote me a very formal letter informing me that I would, of course, be obligated to increase my support payments in direct proportion to my raise. Well, about this time I began to get some idea of the corner that bastard was pushing me into, so I called a lawyer friend of mine who said he'd be glad to advise me but he couldn't handle a divorce. I told him about moving to another state and he said to go right ahead and sign nothing.

"I did and the rest of the story is simple. Her local lawyer contacted a lawyer in my new city, who promptly served me with court papers demanding support, but I threw the papers in the wastebasket. My own lawyer friend told me to just keep sending the money and not worry about anything. I guess that since he wasn't getting a fee himself he was not about to get involved.

"Before I knew it, I was arrested and thrown into jail for nonpayment of support. It took a week and a half before the company lawyer where I worked could study the case, contact my wife's lawyer, bribe the judge, and get me out of jail. Then he warned me that if this ever happened again, I would lose my job immediately. Well, I was so stunned that I just signed everything that was put in front of me and I hope I never see a lawyer or a judge again."

This account can be criticized as being too simplified, but it does illustrate the helplessness of a man when the legal fraternity gangs up on him.

"But Not All Lawyers Are Stinkers . . ."

It is interesting to study the reaction of men and women whose infidelities have led them into contact with lawyers.

Even when their experiences have been pleasant, they often resent the price they have had to pay for very dubious services. (Contrary to popular belief, wives are just as eager as husbands to shed unhappy marriages with a minimum of formality and expense.) The conscientious, intelligent attorney can speed through an uncontested divorce but there always is the possibility that opposing counsel will be a shyster.

A general rule of thumb, according to most divorced persons consulted, is to hire an attorney who does not specialize in divorce cases, and encourage the spouse to do the same. This applies to uncontested divorce in which both partners want to end the marriage with as little trauma as possible. If, however, your spouse is going to play dirty, then by all means shop around for the nastiest, meanest divorce attorney in the area. But before unleashing him, demand a written statement of how much his fee will be and what it will and will not include. He may protest against putting such a delicate matter in writing, but remind him that the experience of divorced men and women strongly indicates that such a policy protects both client and attorney.

The other urgent piece of advice offered by the experienced is that it is safe to follow your lawyer's advice only up to the point where it violates your sense of personal decency and fair play.

Even when both attorneys are honest, it still is true that the only person who wins in a divorce is the lawyer. He gives up none of his property, his income, or his self-respect. He's handsomely paid for his time, and after the case is over he might well join opposing counsel for a drink and perhaps dinner.

Chapter Nine

DIVORCE AND THE INDIVIDUAL

When infidelity ends up in divorce the effect on both individuals can be shattering. It can be extremely unpleasant when it is discovered, but the moment it moves from the privacy of the home into public, the self-respect and reputations of both partners often are severely battered. The truly fortunate are those men and women who don't give a damn about what their friends, relatives, neighbors, or business colleagues think about their personal matters. The individual who is susceptible to social pressure can suffer in agony for months and even years.

Although infidelity itself rarely is the *cause* of a divorce, it often is the trigger. A husband or wife who has attempted to remain monogamous in a marriage that is worsening can experience shock and bitterness on discovering that the spouse has been involved extramaritally. This shock often is accompanied by both anger and personal shame. When a husband and wife open their private emotions to the publicity of a divorce, all emotions can be amplified a thousandfold.

Social Embarrassment

Regardless of which partner is extramaritally involved, the public nature of separation and divorce is bound to bring social embarrassment and humiliation to both, if they so permit it. Friends and relatives immediately want to know all the details, and unless both husband and wife are tight-lipped, word soon spreads among all their acquaintances. Often they are surprised to learn that virtual strangers in the neighborhood or where they work know that the marriage is disintegrating and that infidelity is involved. It is awkward to attend parties where people sidle up and slyly ask intimate questions, pumping hard in order to be able to regale their own friends with details. It is worse when a friend of the separated mate comes up at a party and very nicely tells off the partner present in front of other people. In social groups where both husband and wife are active, one or both usually drop out so as not to give their friends an opportunity to cross-examine them together and perhaps provoke them into an outburst.

Joe and Gerry were a popular couple who both were active in an experimental theater group. They were so active that they constantly were thrown together with interesting, stimulating people of the same age range (they were in their mid-thirties). They got along well publicly, although they didn't spend too much time together when involved with the group. Joe was financially comfortable, having inherited a bustling little business which he was able to run without too much effort. Gerry dressed nicely but without flashiness and both flirted casually and self-confidently whenever someone interested them. They regarded themselves as modern and enlightened, and had they been living in a different setting, they might have entertained the idea of permissive infidelity. Joe frequently found himself teetering on the brink of extramarital affairs but he smilingly declined to become seriously involved. Gerry, on the other hand, was used to being pursued by men but she usually defused them before anything got too serious. One night at a cast party, she got quite giddy on the champagne punch and flirted openly with the leading man, a handsome engineer who was separated from his wife and known to be on the prowl. Other members of the group giggled about it for a few days, gossiping about how Gerry and Steve had wandered into the garden for several hours. When they returned, both appeared rumpled but not enough to cause serious speculation. Knowing Gerry, the other members of the group assumed that this was one more tease.

A month later, at the next cast party, Gerry showed up with Steve, and when someone asked her where Joe was, she replied that they were separating. Within six months they were divorced, and within a year Gerry had married Steve. During that time, Joe quietly dropped out of the group and moved to an apartment near where his business was located. Joe retained his membership but never showed up at any meetings or cast parties. Gerry stayed away for several months, as did Steve, but as soon as they were married, both returned to accept the congratulations of their colleagues and friends. Everyone's questions about what had really happened were deflected smoothly by Gerry, and since Joe was not around, the curiosity of the group had to go unslaked.

Joe's story sheds some light on what actually happened.

"We both worked hard at the image of the compatible, swinging couple, but our marriage had been shaky for years. Since we had no children, we were able to divert ourselves with the theater. I wasn't at all surprised that Gerry fell for Steve, because it seemed just a matter of waiting for the right man to come along and fetch her. For me to have gone back to the group would have meant looking at dozens of friends who knew that my wife had been stolen from me, presumably by a better man. And while I don't dislike Steve, I certainly don't regard him as a superior man. My failing was that while I could give Gerry a very comfortable living and a reasonably pleasant sex life, there was something lacking, and I think this must have been excitement. Whenever we would go out together, I always sensed her straining at the leash, wanting to find someone exciting who would sweep her off her feet, dazzle her with his intelligence and wit, and not leave her any time to think about herself. I thought the theater was safe because most of the men involved were highly talented but lacked the dash and flamboyance that appealed to Gerry. I know that several of them got interested in her and started to chase, but she told me every time she turned one of them off.

"I sensed that something was wrong when Gerry clammed up and told me nothing about Steve. I knew she was at last getting seriously involved, but I didn't think it would last so I didn't worry too much. You see, Gerry comes on as a sweet, sensuous woman who is just full of love which she wants to give to some man. I know, because that's how she came on when we first met. Well, I was confident that after a few weeks, Steve would see through her facade that she really is a strong-willed, somewhat spoiled, self-centered woman whose sensuousness really is a screaming demand for her own sexual satisfaction and the hell with her partner. But I guess Steve is a little dumber than I had thought. Or maybe he is better suited for her than I ever was.

"When she told me about wanting to get a divorce, I knew then that one of us would have to break free from the theatrical group. I wasn't anxious to volunteer, because I have many close friends there, but if we both kept attending it would be humiliating and degrading to one or both of us. We talked about this at some length, and at her suggestion we invited a few close friends over to seek their advice. No sooner had they heard that we were splitting up, these friends immediately began peppering us with questions. The next day, I received five phone calls at the office from other friends who had heard the whole lurid story and wanted more details. At that, I agreed to drop out, secretly wondering how well Gerry would handle the inquisitors. Since our divorce, I still run into some social embarrassment whenever I attend a party where any of our mutual friends are present. They all seem to think they have a right to probe into my private life and lecture me on how I should have kept my marriage together. It is not my nature to tell such people to shove it. I know I should, but I don't. So I had to just make sure that I didn't run into any of them, with the result that for more than a year after the divorce I became a virtual hermit, seeing only my close friends and avoiding all large parties."

"Hell Hath No Fury . . ."

One of the liabilities of infidelity when it contributes to divorce is that it can leave the offended spouse with a thirst for vengeance. A man or woman whose mate has been unfaithful often wants to make him or her suffer, preferably painfully and hopefully in public.

When a husband's extramarital activities have been detected, a wife who is seeking a divorce may well avenge the insult by trying to get him fired from his job, louse up his credit rating, discredit him sexually to anyone who will listen, reveal any personal idiosyncracies, or ruin his business. An offended husband can be every bit as vindictive (there is some evidence to indicate that a spiteful husband can be nastier than a wife). He can denounce her to their friends as an incompetent mother and a ludicrous housekeeper. Their friends will savor the news that she is frigid or just bad in bed. He too can damage her credit rating by warning all local merchants that he will not be responsible for any bills she runs up at their stores. If she takes more than one drink an evening (especially if he is a light drinker), he can portray her as an alcoholic who should not have custody of the children. When her sexual appetite is stronger than his, he often delights in describing her as insatiable, a nymphomaniac lusting after his friends and all the men she meets.

One of the nastiest revenges either husband or wife can exact is to turn the children against the spouse. When the differences have been mutual, this can be difficult to achieve, for once they are old enough to know what is going on, children can determine quickly that both parents are contributing to the breakup. The diplomatic child, faced with two parents who are each denouncing one another, will agree with each separately. However, the truly vindictive husband or wife asks the mate to cooperate in "keeping the children out of this," then proceeds to fill them full of hate for the other parent. When one parent is unaware of what is happening, this scheme can succeed to the point where a child tells the ignorant parent that he doesn't want to see that parent or spend any time with him. Fortunately, such deception of children usually is short-lived, and the child rapidly discovers that the insidious parent has behaved contemptuously. Mothers who hate their ex-husbands enough to attempt this form of vengeance tend to wind up whining that they have given their love to children who now hate them.

WHEN SOMEONE ELSE IS WAITING

Practitioners of infidelity report that nothing is quite so excruciating as being seriously involved with another person who expects them to get out of their marriage immediately. Many such husbands and wives do rush through divorces—prodded, goaded, and nagged by the man or woman waiting in the wings. But a large number who might have been planning divorce balk at this pressure and let the affair disintegrate. They may still divorce, but not just to satisfy someone who is waiting.

The person who is waiting, known familiarly in literature as The Other Man or The Other Woman, can be single, divorced, or unhappily married, and this Other Person can suffer intensely. When the gamble has not been successful, the result usually is bitterness, sometimes remorse.

"I was stupid enough to fall in love with a married man before he was quite ready to leave his wife and family," a thirty-year-old divorcée reports. "He told me he wanted me and was going to move immediately. But he didn't, and as the weeks stretched into months, then into a year, I became increasingly despondent. I suppose I leaned on him too hard, for he suddenly started to collapse physically and emotionally under the strain. Between that bitch he was married to and me he was under fierce pressure, and I finally had to break off with him to preserve my own sanity. About six months later, he did leave his wife, but when I met him for the first time since our breakup, he cut me cold and was barely civil."

A different view is provided by George, a forty-two-year-old engineer who now is happily married a second time.

"When my first wife and I were nearing the end of our marriage, I was desperate for love, and I discovered that a girl I had been very fond of for years, Jillie, was equally unhappy, or so I thought. We fell in love, had an intense affair, and agreed that we really needed each other. It seemed that we couldn't do anything wrong together. She made me proud to be a man, and I functioned superbly in bed to an extent that I had never believed possible and which all the sexual experts say is unlikely for a male of my age. And I did things to her that she said no man had ever come close to achieving. We liked the same movies, music, and plays. Knowing that she had decided to leave her husband, I was delighted that there was something nice and dear waiting for me once I got through the awfulness of the divorce. She helped me pick out an apartment which she said she would love to live in and make into a home for us both. After several months of seeing her a few nights every week, I asked her when she would be getting out of her marriage. She had been assuring me throughout the period that all she had to do was negotiate final arrangements with her husband through their lawyers before he would move out. Once the divorce was final, she promised, she would move in with me. She couldn't until then, however, because he might try to get custody of their thirteen-year-old daughter who was living temporarily with an aunt for the summer. Her husband finally moved out, but he kept reappearing, hoping for a reconciliation. And when he wasn't showing up, her daughter would return for a visit. After several months of pleading with her to speed up the divorce so that we could be together—I even offered to marry her the day after the divorce became final—I realized that she was incapable of cutting the bonds with her husband permanently. I found this out by accident when I met a friend of her husband's at a party, and he told me how Jillie kept encouraging her husband to come back to see if something still existed between them.

"I finally told Jillie that I didn't want to see her until she was ready to come and live with me full time. We had a tremendous scene over this, and I thought that she might repeat her clinging tactics on me as she had been doing with her husband, so I cut it cold. I didn't call her and I wouldn't answer my phone at home or return any calls she made to me at the office."

Those interviewed for this book agreed that infidelity that is going on while divorce is pending should be kept at a casual or at least a nondemanding level, for the presence of The Other Person in the wings can have a disastrous effect on the cool-headedness necessary to maneuver oneself through the legal and emotional jungles.

Chapter Ten

PRACTICAL COMPLICATIONS OF DIVORCE

The drawn-out process of separation and divorce can have serious complications for men and women who are engaged in extramarital affairs. The most obvious of these is money. The cost of maintaining two residences instead of one, plus the care and feeding of two hungry attorneys, can cripple the extramarital activities of husbands and wives. A wife who is involved with another man while her divorce is in progress may not suffer as much as a husband, simply because it is traditional for men to pick up expenses for dining and entertainment. However, a wife who now must watch every penny she receives from her estranged husband cannot be as carefree in her affairs as she might have been before the separation. That is, if she is working, she cannot stay out as late at night as she might wish, and if she has to pay baby-sitters herself this is a powerful impetus to get home earlier. If her ex-husband's income isn't terribly high, she may find herself having to borrow from her boyfriend, a situation which can quickly cool the strongest male ardor. Even if the Other Man is available and eager to marry her, when he sees how much it actually costs to support her and any children she may have, he might conclude that he would be better off pursuing single women or childless divorcées.

The financial pinch of divorce on infidelity is felt acutely by the husband who has moved out. Many ex-husbands claim that the drain on their resources is so great that it denies them the opportunity to seriously pursue women. There is nothing less conducive to a flaming romance than a sudden budgetary cutback and an announcement that instead of eating out every night, they're going to have to cook up some low-cost meals in his one-room apartment, entertainment to be provided by the television set. The Other Woman may be earning a good salary but she may also see that should she marry the man, part of her salary may be commandeered to support his ex-wife and children. And if she wants to have a family herself, the prospect of her children having to do with less than those from his first marriage can sour her rapidly.

One of the tragedies about the alimony and child support system is that it makes husbands too poor to remarry, and it keeps wives from remarrying and losing the alimony. Thus, both continue to suffer from a mistake made in a romantic haze years earlier, and they may suffer for the rest of their lives. This of course is precisely what the framers of our divorce laws had in mind. If you want to get out of marriage, fine, but you're going to suffer for it.

It must be remembered that all the current misery surrounding marriages that haven't worked can be traced back to the puritan ethic, and then back to some of the more astounding moral imbecilities unloaded on mankind by the world's religions. Moralists start with the premise that that which is pleasurable is evil.

Sexual gratification is immensely pleasureable and therefore enormously evil. But since it is a basic need, the moralists decided that it should be permissible only when stripped of as much pleasure as possible. That is, it can only be indulged in without sin after a man and woman take solemn vows and sign legal documents swearing to be monogamous to one another for the rest of their lives. Once married, a couple could be permitted to savor the joys of sex. But intercourse also results in children, so this gave the moralists another lever with which to restrict man's enjoyment of his appetite. Nothing must be permitted to interfere with conception, so the couple that enjoys sex will quickly be saddled with swarms of children.

But what happens when a couple discovers that they are not happy together? Another wrinkle in the moralist's forehead decreed that divorce would be permissible, but no remarriage. Or if remarriage was to be tolerated then divorce would have to be surrounded with every legal and religious unpleasantness to discourage the mob from practising it casually.

Curiously, the theologians who have transmitted Divine Wisdom to mankind about sexual rules and regulations have always been heartily seconded by their brethren in the legal profession. Theologians decree and lawyers legislate and enforce these decrees.

Today, however, even Catholics practise contraception and get divorces without fear, an indication that the old superstitions at last are disappearing. However, the legal restrictions still exist to hamper and cripple those who ignore the theological bans.

Men Who Cannot Afford Alimony

Because each judge is a law unto himself and because divorce court is regarded as the least pleasant judicial assignment, the terms of a contested divorce can vary according to the whim, prejudice, or concern of the individual judge. When infidelity is involved on the husband's part, a puritanical judge might sock the husband with punitively high alimony and child support costs. The mother who admits having an extramarital affair may suffer the wrath of a righteous judge by losing custody of her children or being denied enough money to support them.

The capriciousness of judges in enforcing their own moral codes on divorcing husbands is directly responsible for driving many men into hiding or out of the country. The majority of men who go through divorce are willing to support their children, but only a minority of them are eager to continue supporting their wives after they have severed the marriages, reasoning that she can take care of herself just as she did before marriage. A woman who must raise small children may not want to return to work to support herself, and the richer her ex-husband is, the more likely it is that the courts will soak him for alimony and child support.

The husband who is obliged by a court to cough up exorbitant monthly sums because his yearly income is higher than the average, is in serious trouble if he loses his job or decides to become self-employed. While many divorce actions contain an escalation clause so that the more the husband makes the more his ex-wife collects, they never contain a clause adjusting monthly payments downwards. The man who has lost his job or who is going through a sudden financial crisis receives no consideration from the courts. He must pay up or go to jail. When the sheriff starts breathing down his neck, such a man occasionally says to hell with it and leaves the country for good, defying his ex-wife and giving himself a chance to get started financially again. If he is in a position to pick up another job quickly, that may work well, to the chagrin of the ex-wife, her lawyer, and the courts.

These men become exiles, afraid to set foot back in the country in fear of being arrested and clapped into jail for nonpayment. By moving out of the country, they forfeit any right to regular visits with their children. If they are leaving a vindictive wife, they may never see their children again. Yet this course is one which many men, harassed by lawyers and courts, have chosen.

"The American judicial system is full of crap and so are the lawyers that live off it," a forty-seven-year-old exile claims. "I was reamed purple by a lawyer who was sleeping with my ex-wife, a judge who was appointed by the Mafia, and a set of laws designed by the most corrupt men in our society, the politicians. When I saw this vast antisocial conspiracy moving in on me, I just hopped a plane for Canada, where I was fortunate enough to be able to pick up a job paying me just as much as I was making in the U.S. My only regret is that I cannot demand to see my children. Once I had a brother-in-law sneak them up to see me, but my loving ex-wife found out about it and got an injunction against him. And you know, all the laws are against me. I've regularly sent my wife support money, as much as I could afford, but until I'm willing to pay enough money to support the children, her, and her current lover, I cannot return to the United States. And even if I do make enough to meet the court order, some horse's ass of a judge could clap me in irons for contempt of court."

At the other end of the divorce nightmare is the woman who is afraid to form any close relationship with another man for fear that her ex-husband will catch her and try to cut off alimony and support, or even try to get the children away from her.

Although once the divorce becomes final and her ex-husband no longer exercises any legal claim on her, a divorcée can be attacked in court by him as an unfit mother. This fear can lead women to be ultra-cautious in getting close to other men. Several women report that their ex-husbands have hired private detectives to follow them with cameras and tape recorders in order to trap them in compromising situations with men. A potential second husband, faced with such harassment, might well withdraw completely, especially if he himself is vulnerable in a separation or divorce situation.

The marriage that has been terminated after the appearance of infidelity may not be completely dissolved by the court action. One partner may continue to hang on, either through hope or a desire for revenge. This is particularly true in a small town or a closely-knit community where both partners are well-known. An ex-husband can pick up the phone and get a detailed report on his ex-wife's comings and goings, including how often she has been seen with a man. When a man is seen to enter her house but not emerge, the ex-husband thirsting for revenge may scamper off to his lawyer with tales of unfettered debauchery in front of *his* children.

The man whose children come to visit him periodically may find himself threatened by his wife or her lawyer if he should entertain a woman in front of them. A simple evening together can rapidly escalate into an orgy in the willing imagination of an ex-wife.

There is no handy code of behavior to govern all these possibilities, for they arise out of each individual case. A lawyer who occasionally handles divorces and who himself has gone through such a dissolution, offers one general suggestion.

"If there has to be a divorce, let it be clean and let it be final. Work out a detailed separation agreement that clearly spells out money, property, and other arrangements. Visitation rights must be down in black and white, but they can be stretched according to the goodwill of each party. But once the divorce is decreed, let that be it.

Don't leave any loose ends hanging, for they only prolong discussions. Each person should regard himself as free to make a new life without any thought of the other. If they can't break the ties, then they probably shouldn't get a divorce but rather should work out some system of permissive infidelity until they are ready to split up."

The desire to break free seems to come in waves, according to those interviewed for this study. If the first serious disruption passes, the next spasm may not come again for a few years. Often, the first one is resisted and the two persons make an effort to revitalize the marriage. If there has been no significant repair to the marriage, the second or third waves often shatter it. When these subsequent waves are resisted, perhaps because the children are too young or because a couple is heavily in debt, they usually leave serious scars. It is after such a wave that infidelity often is sought by one or both partners. And when infidelity leads to a serious involvement with another person, that can precipitate another crisis in a battle-weary marriage.

A small percentage of couples never divorce but live as though they had, with each going separate ways. In such situations, one person usually is still hanging on with such a powerful grip that the other cannot break away cleanly and without guilt.

Chapter Eleven

THE COMING REVOLUTION IN MARRIAGE

Infidelity in its traditional sense of adultery only is a slowly dying concept. Those who have been married for many years but who engage in occasional infidelities will continue to do so, just as will all those men and women who regard marriage as a sacred institution yet who have strong unfulfilled needs. For many, infidelity in its various forms is still preferable to divorce.

But for others, whose numbers are increasing every day, the old concepts of marriage, fidelity, and monogamy are no longer sufficient. Men and women who may have subscribed to these concepts when they married are discovering their ineffectualness in helping two people live in harmony together.

A large percentage of the individuals interviewed for this book said they no longer regard infidelity as something to feel guilty about. Nor is it something they wish to avoid.

"It's the nature of the beast for some people," a thirty-two-year-old married woman declared. "It's not even a question of need. Some people just instinctively cannot remain sexually or emotionally monogamous. It's not some great traumatic need-fulfillment for me but simple fun. I like to go to bed occasionally with someone other than my husband. I like to form close attachments with other men. Ten years ago I would have been ostracized by my friends (if I told them what I was doing—which I wouldn't have!), but today I find many men and women who agree with me. My husband's sister is one of them, and although I don't think my husband has played around outside of the marriage, I wouldn't be embarrassed or ashamed to admit to him that I have. I haven't told him simply because I don't want to hurt him because he's a nice man.

"I feel the same way about infidelity as I do about contraception—it's my own business, something between me and the man I'm with. If I want to conceive a child, I shall, but if I conceive by accident, I'll sure as hell get an abortion.

"When I expressed these views to my cousin last week, she denounced me as being amoral. I don't think I am. It's just that I and many, many others have decided to live our own lives and to hell with anyone who tries to tell us how to live them! My body is mine to use as I see fit, and as long as I cause no harm to anyone else, who is to tell me that I am wrong?"

This ebullient manifesto captures the spirit of the coming revolution in marriage. Premarital sex is established, as is premarital contraception and abortion. All that remains to be completely liberated is extramarital activities. This may take a while, for it involves prying man loose from one of his dearest delusions: Monogramy is essential to the survival of modern civilization.

That this change has started and enjoys considerable acceptance can be seen in the replies to a research questionnaire sent out by *Psychology Today* and reported in the July, 1970, issue. More than 20,000 readers returned the questionnaire, leading the editors to observe:

Not as many respondents approve of extramarital sex as they do of sex before marriage. Even so, those who hold that extramarital sex is "wrong whatever the reason" are a minority: about one in five. That leaves almost 80 percent who say that it is all right in various circumstances. More than 20 percent, for example, think that it is permissible if husband and wife agree. However, the "deception" theory—that infidelity is all right if you don't talk about it—is almost totally rejected.

Another interesting observation from the survey is that wives start extramarital affairs later in marriage than husbands. "Once they start, however, women have about the same *frequency* of extramarital intercourse as men."

Why Young People Marry

Perhaps the most refreshing harbinger of this coming liberation is the fact that young people today, unlike their elders, do not need to marry to establish a sex life. Premarital sex has been around for many hundreds of years, but today it is not only common but out in the open. Up until the 1960's, premarital sex was frowned on and those who indulged did so in private, but there were exceptions to this rule. Today, however, it is assumed that a bride and groom who have been through college have either slept together or with other partners. Those who haven't seem to be the exceptions. This statement does not apply to every community, particularly rural or farm towns. Even in these areas, however, physicians are prescribing oral contraceptives for the high school girls, with or without their parents' permission.

What is happening today is that men and women no longer need to be driven into marriage to experience sexual fulfillment. Girls no longer "save it" for marriage because foolproof contraception, combined with social acceptance of premarital intercourse, enables them to develop complete relationships—emotional and physical—with boys before marriage. And young men, no longer sandbagged into marriage as the only outlet for their passions, do not feel the need to brag about their virgin brides and the advantages of marrying a girl who has been "pure."

"Why shouldn't men and women learn whether they are sexually compatible before marriage?" a twenty-three-year-old wife asks. "If I had married the first man I fell in love with I would have been divorced within a year. Or I might have had children and then would have been stuck with a man I couldn't stand for the rest of my life. Rolf and I became seriously involved during my freshman year at college. There was no question about love, but when I think back about it, this really was my first experiment in profound attachment to a man. I suppose if I had been born ten or twenty years earlier I would have married him. However, I obtained a prescription for oral contraceptives and we made love frequently. It was nice, but there were certain things about Rolf that turned me off. The act of making love was very lovely, but after a while, I discovered that he really wasn't doing much to satisfy me. What at first was an act of love grew to be a ritual of passion. Had we been married, I would have been reaching for the marriage manuals and trying to figure out what was wrong with me, why I was frigid, why I couldn't respond to my husband. But we weren't married, and after a few months, I broke up with him.

"The second really important man in my life was my history professor, an extraordinarily sensitive man. Sure, he was married and he was having troubles at home, but we had a wonderful three months together. I thought about marrying him, even though he was twelve years older than I was, and we played little games about being a sedate married couple on some dull midwestern campus and attending faculty teas, then quietly returning to our apartment where we would rip off each other's clothes and make passionate love for hours and hours. This man taught me so much about physical love that I'll never forget him.

"The third major love was Ernest, a boy my age who had been through a succession of girl friends but had not found a satisfying love. Our affair grew slowly, but it prospered for almost a year, to the point where several mutual friends asked when we would be married. Ernest wanted to get married, but I knew I wasn't ready. This difference touched off several fights between us, with him sensing my reluctance yet attempting to overcome it. His idea of marriage was one of strict monogamy, with me staying home minding the children and cleaning the house while he worked each day as the junior junior partner in a law firm, slowly rising to the top so that by the time we both were sixty, he'd be a top lawyer and I'd be a grandmother, and we'd both spend evenings together looking through scrapbooks and maybe occasionally making love.

"By the time I graduated, I knew what I wanted in a husband, and I knew exactly how to find it. I spent a year working in various jobs and attending graduate school nights before I met a man I wanted to investigate as a potential husband. Bill had had extensive experience with women and we both moved together very casually. After spending several months dating, sleeping together, and arguing, I decided that this was a man that I could marry and stay with for a few years. Around the same time, Bill reached the same decision, and so we married.

"I feel that I have been fortunate in selecting a husband carefully, and I feel sorry for all my friends who leaped into marriage with the first man who turned them on. Bill is no more the perfect husband than I am the perfect wife, but we do get along nicely. By living with him before marriage, I resolved most sexual questions, and as a result I'm delighted when we make love.

"Maybe another man will come along who will really light my fires even more than Bill does, but if that happens I'll worry about it then. And he feels the same way."

ACCEPTANCE OF INFIDELITY

As premarital sex becomes not only tolerated but expected, the rigid social abhorrence of infidelity is loosening up a bit. That is, infidelity always has existed, but until very recently it has been violently denounced by all right-thinking people, especially those who are practising it. In recent years, observers of marriage have started to suggest that infidelity might actually be beneficial to marriage. Of course, these observations are heavily qualified to include only very occasional infidelity.

Looking beyond the marriage counselors, psychiatrists, and psychologists—who, after all, are talking about other people's marriages and not their own—it is useful to listen to the opinions of the men and women who, for many different reasons, are defying monogamy.

To a person, they defend infidelity. For some it is preventive therapy to keep pressures from building in marriage. For others, it is an alternative to divorce. For even more, it is a pleasure and a joy to be indulged in for its own sake.

Not only do they defend infidelity, these men and women insist that it is widespread, particularly in its emotional and psychological manifestations. Husbands and wives can get involved extramaritally with great ease today, and as they get involved more and more, they are increasingly unhappy with the social and moral stigma attached to what they are doing.

"Why must infidelity be a dirty word in marriage?" a well-practised wife asks. "Last year, I became so sick of this hypocritical society that I decided to start being an honest person. My husband had been discussing our oldest daughter's new boyfriend, speculating on whether she would end up in bed with him. He seemed to think nothing of premarital sex so I announced to him that, as far as I was concerned, extramarital sex and love is not only enjoyable, but it is completely liberated. He was shocked, but then, when he thought I was just speaking theoretically, he relaxed and decided to humor me. He asked if what I said applied to him and I said of course. He's a nice man and so sensitive that I couldn't punch him in the nose with the fact that I intended to have affairs. I had no intention of mentioning the men I have been involved with but I did want to clear the boards of any pretense. I couldn't get through to him, perhaps because he deliberately is refusing to listen to me."

Many individuals who are on second or third marriages report that a thorough agreement is necessary before marriage so that there is no misunderstanding or hurt feelings after the ceremony. When the new husband and wife are equally experienced with monogamy, such agreement seems to be easier to obtain than with one who has not been married or has come from a marriage in which everything was rotten.

Agreement is almost impossible when two persons married with monogamy in mind but one has since discovered the mistake. Just being honest is not always the answer, for such a policy might easily offend the spouse deeply.

But to practise infidelity while keeping it covered up is, to many, intensely upsetting. What is the answer to this unpleasant dilemma? There is none, except possibly broader public discussion and acceptance of infidelity as a fact of married life, not a phenomenon.

What it narrows down to for many married persons is the question of whether marriage confers power over another person's body and emotions. A surprisingly large majority of the men and women interviewed for this book expressed almost identical attitudes on this subject. They were openly hostile to the concept that a marriage certificate grants to anyone else the right to dictate what the individual does with his or her body or emotions. What possible logic dictates to an intelligent human being that he can eat when he is hungry, drink when he is thirsty, sleep when he is tired, relieve himself when the need arises, and exercise his body when it becomes weak and flabby—but must not indulge his sexual appetite except with one person and under rigidly controlled conditions? Notice the word *intelligent* in the last sentence. It is to be expected that the less gifted of the human species will surround their bodily functions with absurd rituals, but the detached observer of human behavior must wonder at the way he restricts one of his appetites and instincts.

Disregarding the pronouncements of theologians for a moment, marriage is nothing more than an agreement by a man and a woman to live together, perhaps raise children, and establish a mutual home. There is nothing in the agreement (which frequently is called a *contract* to define it as a legally-binding formality) which in any way grants control over mind or body to the other person.

It is interesting to note that the decline of the concept of sexual ownership in marriage is slipping in behind the dramatic change in women's position in marriage. Just within this century, wives have moved to equality with their husbands. Today they have as much to say about the conduct of a marriage as the husband, and often more.

Not only has the wife moved away from the role of servant, housekeeper, social companion, and private whore, but she also has gained sexual equality. She expects sexual satisfaction, a notion that for some reason still outrages a minority of men. Since the development of reliable contraceptives, and particularly since the arrival of the Pill, she has been able to enjoy sex whenever she wants it, without fear of pregnancy. Depending on her age and her attitudes, she may have experimented sexually before marriage.

More than ever before, the wife is on equal sexual footing with her husband. If she works, she is exposed to other men, some of them definitely superior to the man she married. She sees other husbands indulging in infidelity, and even if she knows that her husband is monogamous, she cannot help but entertain the thought of extramarital involvement herself.

The leap from the freedom to practise infidelity to actually indulging can be a very small one, and all indications are that modern marriage is moving in that direction.

Revisions of the Marriage Agreement

If infidelity goes the same way as contraception and abortion, years of social pressure and change may be necessary before realistic marriage reforms become legal. Both legal and social codes governing marriage, divorce, and extramarital sex need a thorough revision, simply because the current codes are so frequently ignored.

The major change in these codes is the elimination of

monogamy as a concept. If two persons wish to practise it, that is their privilege. However, for many, many marriages, monogamy is just a silly idea.

We speak of changing legal and social codes. Naturally, a social code will only be changed by extensive exposure of the new idea to practise, such as has happened with premarital sex.

The major legal change to be made is in the divorce laws. There is some progress in that direction, and perhaps within several years it may be possible to dissolve an unsatisfactory marriage swiftly and painlessly.

Perhaps the simplest revision that would do the most long-term good would be to eliminate the *need* for lawyers in breaking up a marriage. At the present time, it is difficult and foolish to divorce without benefit of legal counsel, simply because the person who does not use a lawyer will be roundly raped by the spouse's lawyer.

Infidelity has been practised and recognized for a long time, but it has not been openly acknowledged as an almost inevitable side effect of marriage. To so acknowledge its existence would be an admission that it is a serious symptom of what is wrong with the ancient institution of marriage.

As an institution, marriage is in no danger. It will continue in one form or another. It has survived transitions from polygamy to monogamy, as well as all the liberalizing influences of the twentieth century. Men and women enjoy premarital sex, they control conception, and they can terminate unwanted pregnancies, yet they still marry.

All that is needed is a general awareness that monogamy *today* does not always work and therefore should be scrapped as a *sine qua non* of marriage. The refusal of society to acknowledge that monogamy is a myth, is responsible for infidelity, and all the guilt that surrounds it.

Actually, monogamy is an unnatural state. Of the major animal and bird species, only a few come remotely close to monogamy, but for them it is a question of supply and demand, not morality. It is absurd to presume that one human being can answer all the needs of another human being for the duration of each other's lives. Yet such an absurdity is the foundation of monogamy. There is no question that at a given moment, only one person may be capable of answering the particular need of another. Man, with his indefatigable yen to regulate and institutionalize, erroneously reasons that if monogamy works today, it should continue to work tomorrow.

Over the course of hundreds of hours of interviews and conversations about infidelity, one strong plea has been repeated over and over again: Infidelity is the human rebellion against an impossible ideal of monogamy and must be freed from notions of sin and guilt. Two human beings, no matter how deep their love, cannot be all things to one another, and when internal pressures force them to look outside of marriage for fulfillment, they should be able to do so as free individuals, unfettered by guilt. Man has enough antisocial traits to be guilty about without having to deny his instincts to draw close to another human. Extramarital involvements are less objectionable than murder, war, and persecution. Infidelity, even in its most guilt-ridden form, has kept men and women from going insane in difficult marriages. In its less-restricted forms, it has steadied good marriages, hurried the dissolution of rotten unions, inspired great literature, and moved men and women to enjoy life. It has brought happiness to those who otherwise might have shuffled unpleasantly through life. Infidelity also has helped men and women decide whether or not they are fit for marriage, bypassing the social platitude that all should marry.

The Future

Those who sneer that marriage cannot be changed and that acknowledgement of infidelity would lead to a social disaster are wrong. Institutions even more tradition-ridden than marriage have survived stunning revolutions. A nineteenth-century Everyman would have hooted at the idea that a man would ever have sexual relations with a woman before marriage and then marry her—unless her father held a shotgun to his head. In polite society, men only copulated with whores or with "fallen women." He also would have dismissed with scorn the idea that wives would one day be equal to their husbands, not only running the household and family but also working competitively alongside men.

Such a man, it should be pointed out, would also have howled at the idea of airplanes, nuclear bombs, and heart transplants.

Just for a bit of variety, let's take Everyman and move him in time to 1950. We'll tell him that within a generation one of the oldest, most calcified institutions, the Roman Catholic Church, would purge its liturgy of Latin, greatly modify the Mass, permit long-haired youngsters to play electric guitars and drums during services, and entertain suggestions that priests be permitted to marry. His laughter would be earsplitting.

Anyone who believes that the institution of marriage is too sacred, too rigid to change would be well advised to examine the history of the Catholic Church in recent years. Here was a world power, a phenomenon unique in the history of Western Civilization which, within a few years during the 1960's, kicked over centuries of tradition and, despite the howls of traditionalists, modernized its liturgy, fired several dubious saints, and openly admitted the silliness of some of its dogma.

If the Catholic Church could change so radically in such a brief period, there is hope for marriage. A person's marital life is as important to him as his religious beliefs, and the fact that millions of Catholics have been able to accept changes in their religion might be a sign that marriage is the next institution to be liberated.

And when it finally is free of the shackles of monogamy, infidelity will become a part of man's past, just as heresy no longer horrifies believers.

Infidelity is indeed part of the way we live today. We are just beginning to recognize the extent to which infidelity has pushed monogamy. Infidelity is a mirror that shows us exactly what marriage is. It also shows us what monogamy has done to marriage. But this is a reflection we have been trying not to look at for years. So we call the reflection evil, pretend it doesn't exist, outlaw it in the pulpit and in the legislature. But it's still there and always will be there.

Epilogue

If after finishing this book, the reader is depressed, I would not be at all surprised, for that was my own reaction when I finished the final draft. However, it would be wrong to conclude this study on a gloomy note.

There is much sadness in infidelity, but there also is much joy. The concept of monogamy has, as its base, an inexhaustible supply of guilt for whomever violates it. But monogamy is no longer universally accepted, and during my researches I found many men and women who experience no guilt from infidelity.

One question which this book has not attempted to answer is what makes a good marriage. Since this question was not one I was asking the practitioners of infidelity to answer, I can only offer a subjective opinion.

A good marriage seems to be one in which monogamy is in no way involved, particularly as a moral issue. It may in fact exist much of the time, but it is tolerated voluntarily. In the very few good marriages I have seen, both partners manage to keep themselves active, creative, and productive for several hours a day. They each have their own friends, plus some mutual friends. They look to each other, not for constant attention, conversation, reassurance, or admiration, but rather for love and the closeness that two persons can give one another.

Perhaps the single key to successful marriage is for each partner to be completely self-assured and self-confident. Sexual compatibility helps and so does a common agreement on such topics as money and raising children. For each partner to remain exciting to the other is an ideal that everyone would like to preserve, yet the nature of marriage, with its stripping away of facades and its exposure of personal flaws, is destructive to this ideal.

A questionable ingredient in a successful marriage is what has been described in this book as permissive infidelity. It is questionable only because it too often is employed grudgingly, or just by one partner, or after the marriage has already foundered. When it is genuinely endorsed by both partners, it seems to provide the answer to what is needed to keep a marriage together.

Of course, keeping marriages together is an obsession almost as powerful as the monogamy lobby. My interviews and observations all point to the renewable contract concept of marriage. Some favor a five-year contract, others vote for two-year contracts. In these views, marriage should definitely not be a lifetime bargain, but rather something that can be reevaluated every few years.

Another element for pleasant marriage is to remove it from the controls of Church and State. If it really is the enormously complicated legal partnership that lawyers describe when it has turned sour, then perhaps it should be entered into only on the advice of an attorney. Either that or get lawyers out of the marriage-divorce business altogether. If divorce becomes as easy as marriage, partners who never should have married can remedy that mistake quickly and without guilt.